# Suffering Is Optional

STEP OUT OF DARKNESS INTO THE LIGHT

By

**Michelle Nagel**

Published by
Union Square Publishing
301 E. 57th Street, 4th floor
New York, NY 10022
www.unionsquarepublishing.com

Copyright © 2017 by Michelle Nagel

All rights reserved. No part of this book may be reproduced or transmitted in any form or by in any means, electronic or mechanical, including photocopying, recording, or by any information storage and retrieval system, without the written permission of the Publisher, except where permitted by law.

Manufactured in the United States of America, or in the United Kingdom when distributed elsewhere.

Nagel, Michelle
    Suffering Is Optional: Step Out of the Darkness and Into the Light
    ISBN:
    Paperback: 978-1-946928-02-3
    eBook: 978-1-946928-03-0


Cover design by: Joe Potter
Interior design: Scribe, Inc


www.isoulshift.com

**DEDICATION**

This book is dedicated to the sincere seeker of transformation. You can design the kind of life you previously only dreamed of. May you believe in yourself and discover the joy of intentionally creating change that brings you into alignment with who you really are.

## ACKNOWLEDGEMENTS

I'm sure this book would still a dream if it were not for the loving support of my husband, Jeffrey. After years of talking about writing a book, he was delighted when I began. He is a wonderful sounding board. He had the courage to read the manuscript and tell me where I needed to rewrite something to make it stronger and give it clarity. I didn't always want to hear it, but he was always right. Most especially, I am grateful for the years we have been best friends, lovers, and partners.

My friend and accountability partner, Melinda Irvine, has a gift for telling me just what I need to hear when I need it most. She is a masterful cheerleader with laser-sharp insight. She is so good at making sure I count my wins in my victory notebook because it helps me track my successes and avoid getting overwhelmed by the minute details of day-to-day life.

To my beautiful children, who are all a part of this book. I learned so much from being your mom. I am so impressed by the adults you have become in spite of my inexperience. Thank you for being such amazingly good people. I love you.

I am grateful for the all of the coaches at Quantum Leap, but specifically Geoffrey Berwind, Martha Bullen, and Ann McIndoo and her staff—I don't know what I would have done without you. I am so grateful for your help every step of the way. Thank you for your expertise and willingness to share it.

Huge thanks go to Jack Canfield and his staff for first teaching me the power of the principle of 100% Responsibility and supporting me all along my journey to success.

Thank you, also, to my clients. I love the courage with which you step into redesigning your lives.

# CONTENTS

| | | |
|---|---|---|
| | *Introduction* | 1 |
| 1: | Change | 3 |
| 2: | My Journey | 7 |
| 3: | The Birth of Soul Shift™ | 17 |
| 4: | The Wall: Why We Do the Things We Do | 31 |
| 5: | Survivors of Abuse: Insights to Better Understand Yourself | 53 |
| 6: | Shame: The Darkness Lurking Within | 63 |
| 7: | Self-Perception: The Myth in the Mirror | 71 |
| 8: | Relationships: How to Get Off the Merry-Go-Round | 83 |
| 9: | Addictions | 95 |
| 10: | The Pain Point | 101 |
| 11: | Who Are You Really? Live Your Own Life | 111 |
| 12: | Forgiveness and the Parable of the Horses | 121 |
| 13: | The Desires of Your Heart | 129 |
| 14: | As a Man (or a Woman) Thinketh | 139 |
| 15: | Be a Soul Shifter | 151 |
| | *References* | 157 |
| | *About the Author* | 159 |

# Introduction

This book is a culmination of over 30 years of research, study, and old-fashioned hard work. I have felt so much pain in my own life. It hurt to be me. I never felt like I was good enough. I could never figure out why I couldn't find the happiness I observed in other people. They had happy families, were successful in their lives, and seemed to love life. This had never been my experience, and I felt broken, hopeless, and angry. I felt as if I had been run over by the "semi-trucks of life" one too many times, and I was unable to find the energy to pull myself upright. What had I done to deserve being at the bottom of the world's barrel?

As I studied, I learned how to release my pain. Through long days, months, and years, I finally discovered the "blueprint" for happiness. It wasn't in the circumstances of my life—it was within me. As I changed my internal dialogue and erased the writing on my internal wall, my outside circumstances began to change, as well.

I wrote this book for everyone who is tired of the pain of not being enough. I want to show you the shortcuts I learned so you can move from who you are to who you want to be much faster than I did.

If you use the techniques in this book with diligence, you will feel that *ka-chunk* of recognizing that your life has shifted in a profound way. When you feel the Soul Shift, you are already well on your way to finding the happiness that has eluded you.

The Shift is within.

CHAPTER ONE

# Change

> I can't change the direction of the wind, but I can adjust my sails to always reach my destination.
>
> —*Jimmy Dean*

The human mind is an amazing thing. With it, we strive to control our environment, influence others around us, and try to interpret our own responses to the world. What seems to make us so unique is our spirit.

For centuries people have made reference to the spirit of mankind. One's spirit can be broken. One can be high-spirited. There is the old adage, "The spirit is willing, but the flesh is weak."

Spirit is what makes us individuals. We may share similar characteristics with someone else, such as looks, behaviors, etc., but no one is exactly like anyone else. There is some defining spark that makes each one of us unique.

Like animals, humans have the ability to "read" or discern the spirit of another person. Just as some animals take an instant dislike to a person, no matter how nice they appear to be on the outside, we can be aware that there is something "off" or "wrong" about someone, and we are wary. On the other hand, there are some people we are instantly drawn to.

We want to be close to them because of the way we feel when we are around them.

One of the most glorious things about being human is that we are able to make conscious choices. As we go through life, we are able to choose how we will respond or react to situations. Some of us do this more deliberately than others, but everyone, no matter their circumstance, is able to either respond or react.

Responding is more powerful than reacting. When you *respond* to something, you choose your behavior. You are in control of yourself, even if you aren't able to control your environment, or a situation that you may find yourself in.

A *reaction* is instantaneous, without thought. Sometimes that can be life-saving, as when you see danger and get out of the way, and sometimes it can create a disaster, as when you strike out and hit someone because you were startled or frightened.

One of the most important lessons I have learned is that everyone is doing the best they can do at all times with the knowledge and tools at their disposal. Choosing to believe that has made such a difference in my life. Now, rather than getting upset at the person driving down the street like a maniac, I am able to observe, "Wow, they sure are driving like a maniac," choose my response, "I'd better slow down so we're not in the same space," and send them on their way with good thoughts, "Go with God—I hope you make it safely to wherever you're going in such a hurry."

I don't know what's going on with them. Maybe they just got a message that a family member was rushed to the hospital, and they're trying to get there as fast as they can. I once observed a woman sobbing uncontrollably as she was weaving in and out of traffic, and sent a quick prayer in her direction. I have done that myself, sobbing and driving when trying to get away from a dangerous situation. It wasn't a great choice to make, but it seemed to be the only one I had at the time. It is not a choice I would make today. In that small way, I have changed.

Change goes by many names: adjustment, metamorphosis, transformation, reversal, repentance, etc. It is often accompanied by emotional and spiritual pain and anguish as a person stretches and grows into something better, or shrinks and collapses into something worse. It is something we all do to fit in with a group or feel better about ourselves.

The ability to make conscious choice is one of the greatest gifts we have. We can choose to redesign our lives if they aren't working for us. Throughout history there have always been tales of people who were evil, then saw the error of their ways and changed.

During my lifetime, I have made many conscious changes. The woman I am today is a far cry from the woman I was in my 20s. I respond more, react less. I like to think I'm a better person today—kinder, more patient, compassionate, and understanding.

I had a friend years ago that said that she moved a lot as a child. She actually liked it, because each new move allowed her to become someone else. If there was a certain behavior that hadn't worked for her at one school, she tried on another one. She said she felt like she was given a blank slate with each move as an opportunity for her to redefine herself without any constraints or expectations, because nobody at the new school knew who she had been. Was she too shy? Next time she tried being more outgoing. She didn't feel that hanging out with a labeled group such as the "skaters," "jocks" or "nerds" was who she really wanted to be, so next time she befriended another group of kids. By the time I knew her, she had evolved into a very gregarious, confident, friendly, compassionate woman whom I greatly admired. She assured me that she had not always been that way, but that she was a work in progress, and the result of deliberate choices.

We all have the power to choose to be different. Just as I have chosen to be different than I was years ago, the people mentioned in this book may also have chosen to be different than they were during the time our lives intersected. In particular, I was frequently told that one of my abusers "had changed." Maybe he did, I don't know. I would hope so, for his sake.

People come and go in our lives every day. Some of them stay around for a long while, perhaps for most of our lives, and others are only fleeting brushes of momentary interaction. Not one of us can go through life without impacting someone else, even if for a brief flash of time.

The people I mention in this book who impacted me throughout my life may have chosen to change or transform their behaviors and thoughts somewhere along the way so that they would be very different today than they were. Just as I claim the right to change, so can they.

It's only fair that I acknowledge it's a possibility.

## CHAPTER TWO

# My Journey

## The Psychologist

Although it was a gorgeous day outside, it felt like deepest winter in my soul. I was in my early 30s and had just returned from yet another appointment with my psychologist. Once again, I had sifted through my traumatic childhood memories, examining the details and trying to understand why my adult life was so painful.

As I recreated those childhood events in my mind, I felt as though I had stepped into a smelly barrel of toxic black ooze, lunging and grasping after slippery unseen answers to the pain that brushed against my fingertips and vanished again into the abyss.

After thrashing around for 50 minutes, my psychologist announced cheerfully, "That was great! I think we really made some progress! I will see you again next week."

As I was ushered out the door, I felt as if I were dripping steaming muck behind me. I cried all the way home. It was this way every week.

It seemed that despite all the time I spent embracing the horror, bringing it into my lap and examining it, nothing changed in my reality. I would spend the entire week trying to overcome the depressing effects of therapy, only to go back the next week and do it all over again.

I was prescribed an antidepressant by my psychiatrist, which I dutifully took until I had an adverse reaction that endangered my family. This event left me shaken and terrified because I felt I could no longer trust myself to keep my family and myself safe. What behavior was mine and what was drug-induced?

The doctor reduced the dosage and reassured me that I would never do anything while taking the medication that I would not do normally. He insisted that some internal mechanism would keep me from harming someone if it was not in my nature.

I didn't believe him. I listened to the news. I was not willing to take the chance that I would be in one of those terrible stories of a mother who did something unspeakable to her family. I demanded to be weaned off the drug.

It was intensely frustrating. I had tried psychotherapy twice now, and nothing seemed to help relieve the emotional pain of a life that just wasn't working.

Ten years earlier, when I was barely into my 20s, I went to a therapist for the first time. She gave me a precious gift. She helped me understand that my childhood experiences had shaped the choices I made. At last, I finally understood why I did the things I did. My choices were often knee-jerk, instinctive reactions that guaranteed I would always remain in the same kind of environment I had been born into. The players might change, but the story never changed. I had been given some precise subconscious instructions by my family of origin that dictated how I felt about myself and what kind of choices I would make in order to maintain the status quo.

Once I understood the reasons behind my behavior, I was able to be more deliberate in my choices. I was not really good at it, but I began trying to craft my own life. However, the harder I tried, the more I realized I didn't have the foggiest idea of what I was doing. Healthy decision-making had never been modeled for me, and I realized I didn't have any tools with which to change.

## My Search Began

After my second attempt at traditional therapy and subsequent pharmaceutical drug reaction, I knew there had to be a better way to be free of my suffering. I did not want to simply put a bandage over my wounded psyche and try to ignore it, so I began searching for change and a way to create personal peace. I did not want to keep dredging up painful memories. I wanted to be rid of them, or at least rid of their ability to haunt and control me.

I am a deeply spiritual person. Along with prayer and study of the scriptures, I read every book I could get my hands on about healing the mind. My bookshelves began to look like the public library, and the excess spilled over onto the floor.

I read John Bradshaw's books *Healing the Shame That Binds You* and *Bradshaw on the Family*. They were the first books I had read that were written in a way I could understand and relate to. While reading, I was amazed to have moments when I thought, *Oh my gosh! This is my life; this happened to me! I recognize myself in his writing.* It gave me hope that I might truly be able to change my life. Just knowing someone understood and could describe what I had experienced and what I was feeling was amazingly freeing.

The second book I relied on heavily was Karol Truman's *Feelings Buried Alive Never Die*. I still keep this book close by as a resource for when I am not able to identify the reason for a health issue I am experiencing.

The majority of illnesses we experience have an underlying emotional component. If I have a pain in my shoulder, I go to *Feelings Buried Alive Never Die*. I look up "shoulders" and read, "Life is too great a burden to bear," or, "bearing burdens that do not belong to you." With this extra bit of information, I am able to look at myself and ask: *Whose burden am I trying to shoulder?* This helps me let go of whatever is not mine or give the burden back to whomever it belongs so I do not have to carry it anymore.

From multitudes of authors, I learned about codependency, enmeshment, and attachment disorders.

Codependency is a dysfunctional relationship characterized by an unhealthy reliance on someone else—a hunger for approval, as well as looking to another person for your very identity. In this type of relationship, one partner supports or enables the other in addictions, immature behavior, poor mental health, and irresponsibility. The codependent person often makes excuses for a partner's poor behavior in order to maintain the relationship.

Enmeshment is like codependency on steroids. When two or more people have no personal boundaries, their emotions can become so intertwined that when one escalates emotionally the other does, too. For example, if a child becomes depressed and anxious, the parent often feels the same way. An enmeshed person might feel they have to rescue someone else from their feelings.

Attachment disorder is when a person fails to form lasting relationships and is unable to be genuinely affectionate or trusting of another. This happens because of failure to form a natural attachment to a caregiver in infancy or childhood. Although attachment disorder can happen in any family, it is more common in families where there is abuse.

Each person assumes a role in the family in order to fit in and feel like they belong. This role can become their entire identity and carry over into new relationships as an adult.

The intricacies of the mind fascinated me, as I discovered there is always more to learn in the study of human psychology.

My search took me to herbs in order to heal the mind and body. I knew my ancestors had used herbs before pharmaceuticals had even been imagined. I attended the School of Natural Healing and graduated with a Master Herbalist degree. I witnessed many amazing things as I taught the traditional and historical use of herbs. When my students chose to use herbs, most of the time the herbs were exactly the support they needed for their health to improve. However, occasionally I observed that someone who chose to take herbs did not get well, no matter how faithfully they followed the usual protocol.

This reinforced my suspicion that there is something much stronger than traditional or alternative medicine. This *something* is the power of the mind and the emotions.

I dove back into the study of emotions and how to process them in a healthy way. I studied SHEN with Richard Pavek and discovered how to use the power of *chi*—the fundamental life force that flows through all and everything—in order to release my trapped emotions. During my study, I experienced profound emotional releases that shifted my entire world. In using this method with my clients, they often express delight at feeling the energy move so powerfully through the areas of their bodies where energy had previously been stagnant. One of my clients described it as feeling like the energy came out of her fingers and toes, much like the transformation the Beast went through in Disney's *Beauty and the Beast*.

SHEN is usually performed while the client is reclining on a massage table. One hand of the practitioner is generally under the client's body; the other is held over the body. After a few years, I found that if a particular client was heavy, some of the positions I had to put my hands in to get the *chi* moving became rather painful for me. I continued searching for a technique that would help release the client's pain at a cellular level, but that was not so physically demanding for me. I discovered that EFT (Emotion Freedom Technique, or tapping) does this quite well. EFT is often called "emotional acupressure." It is a process in which an individual mentally tunes in to specific issues while simultaneously stimulating certain meridian points on the body by tapping on them with the fingertips.

Meridians are the internal energy pathway through which the life force known as "qi" flows. When done correctly, EFT appears to balance disturbances in the meridian system with astonishing results. It can augment traditional therapeutic methods or be used effectively for self-healing. I studied EFT with Gary Craig and some of his masters. Please see the References section at the end of this book for more information.

Next, I studied The Emotion Code and The Body Code with Dr. Bradley Nelson. Dr. Nelson developed both of these systems, and I had great success in moving blockages in my clients using the Emotion Code.

My studies took me from Acupuncture to Zen. Once I had learned how to process my stuffed emotions so my memories had no power to control me, I felt much better. However, I was still unable to make any lasting changes in my life.

I did not know how to move from the generational dysfunction I had been raised with to living a life of my own choosing, a life of my own design, a life I had only dreamed about. In moments of extreme frustration, when it came to determining how to live differently, how to be successful, and how to have more money, I would say to myself, *Michelle, you are a brilliant woman. Why can't you figure this out?*

I really couldn't figure it out. I didn't have the tools, and it really had nothing to do with brilliance but rather knowing the blueprint, or path. I knew there were people who had lives filled with loving relationships. I had observed the family of a good friend and how his parents were engaged in their children's lives. They lovingly interacted with the children and one another; they were supportive while also providing firm guidelines for their family. Somewhere, I knew there had to be instructions on how to achieve something like that! I kept searching.

I began reading Brian Tracy and listening to his audiotapes about positive mindset and successful habits.

I read Barry Neil Kaufman, the cofounder of the Option Institute and author of *Happiness is a Choice*. This phrase became my mantra when things were not going well. When I was feeling depressed or angry or upset, I would remind myself that, "Happiness is a choice, and I choose to be happy!"

I read Napoleon Hill's *Think and Grow Rich*. I had known about this book since I was a teenager, and I was fascinated by the concept that my thoughts could change my circumstances. To me, this idea was the equivalent of flying.

If I could really change my circumstances and my life by regulating the things I thought about, then perhaps I really could get myself out of the poverty of my existence, including the abuse and pain I carried around in my soul because of my childhood.

I read Stephen R. Covey's *Seven Habits of Successful People*, and many, many other talented and inspired authors.

Then I met Jack Canfield, author of the *Chicken Soup for the Soul* books as well as *The Success Principles*. I attended his *Breakthrough to Success* seminar, and became a *Certified Jack Canfield Success Principles Trainer*. Under his expert, personal tutelage over the course of two years, I learned how to accept 100% Responsibility for my life. I also learned how to identify my dreams and passions, and how to implement change in my life—not the kind of change that overtakes a person in the natural course of a lifetime, but intentional change of my own design.

Jack taught me the courage to speak my truth. He took me through difficult exercises that explored my feelings of guilt and resentment so I could let them go. He always pushed me gently to find my truth. Sometimes I hated his pushing. It took me through some very painful territory. Jack is very good at what he does, and he can see through any number of protective barriers a person can devise—and I had devised many.

Taking the best of everything I had learned over the years, I developed a process I call the "Soul Shift," the blueprint, or map I had been searching for. This book will show you how to begin making make this Shift yourself.

## The Soul Shift™ Blueprint

The Soul Shift™ program is a set of specific steps, exercises, and attitude shifts that can help you break free from the internal prison you have built for yourself over the years. Only by taking action can anyone be totally free. It has been said that life is a journey, not a destination. This book is a guide to help you have more control over your journey, discard some of the heavy "stones" in the baggage you (and all of us) carry, and help you choose happiness and joy instead of fear and self-limiting beliefs and behaviors.

The letters in the name "Soul Shift" play an important, integral part in this healing system:

S = Survive
O = Overcome
U = Understand
L = Let Go

S = Strategies
H = Hope
I = Intuition
F = Face Forward
T = Trust God/Trust Yourself

If you are still breathing, you have *Survived* something. Life is full of challenges, struggles, trials, and pitfalls. You have *Overcome* many difficult things to get to the place you are today. Through the pages of this book, as you begin to examine your life, you will *Understand* things about yourself that you might not have known before. Knowledge is power. When you process the emotions from your past and present life, you will finally be able to *Let go*, and this will bring you freedom. You will learn *Strategies* and discover resources that will help you in your growth process. Perhaps for the first time in a long time, you will begin to feel *Hope* as you redesign your life and begin to see results. Rediscovering and trusting your *Intuition* will make such a difference. As you do this work, you will learn to *Face forward*, leaving behind the elements of your past that have controlled you against your will. Conquering the self-doubt that has plagued you in many different forms over the years, you will learn to *Trust God*, and *Trust Yourself*.

In this book, you will read true stories from my own life and from the lives of some of my clients. Their names have been changed to protect their privacy. See if you recognize your own experience in these stories.

In each chapter, there are several questions for you to answer, as well as things for you to think about. I encourage you to do the work. There will be no change if there is no effort. As the late motivational speaker and author, Jim Rohn, once said, "You can't hire someone else to do your pushups for you!"

I am not going to pretend this was an easy process for me, or that change will be easy for you. We live our lives the way we do because it is familiar. We don't like to "rock the boat." Often, the people around us will object strenuously to any attempt we make to change or create healthy habits.

A counselor once told me that my life would get noisier before there was an improvement in my circumstances, because the people around me were likely to push back against any change to the status quo. She was right. It did. However, I made it through, and now I want to help as many people as possible navigate the path to happiness and peace.

Writing this book was the scariest thing I have ever had to do, although I realize it was a choice. I've used the phrase "had to do" because I felt compelled every step of the way. I fought against actually doing it for ten years. I am not a big fan of being vulnerable, and this book feels as though I am baring my soul to the world. I tend to protect myself against this at every turn; however, I have come to learn through the work of Brené Brown that I cannot live a wholehearted life unless I embrace vulnerability, allow others to see it, and just let it be.

I finally accepted the responsibility to write this book for one simple reason: I love you. No, I have probably never met you, but I know you. I have been you. I honor you for your courage to try to change yourself, your circumstances, and your life.

So let us do this Soul Shift together and change the world, one beautiful soul at a time.

CHAPTER THREE

# The Birth of Soul Shift™

> **Definition of Soul:** "The spiritual part of a person that is believed to give life to the body and in many religions is believed to live forever."
>
> —Merriam-Webster.com

If you look up the word "soul" in the dictionary, you are apt to get more definitions than you ever imagined. Put ten people in a room and ask them to define the soul, and you will most likely get ten different answers. You might also find it necessary to separate some of these people, as they might get rather heated in their disagreement with each other's definitions.

So there is no misunderstanding as to my meaning in this book, the definition I use of soul is "the immortal and eternal spirit united with the physical body." Although sometimes our spirits are called "souls," in this book I make a distinction between soul and spirit, and I have tried to maintain consistency.

I believe the soul is eternal, and the spirit and the body together make up the soul. The spirit dwelt with God before the beginning of time. It joins with the mortal body at birth, and at death it is separated from the mortal body and returns to dwell with God—to be reunited with the body at the resurrection. The eternal part of us continues to learn and grow forever.

## How Soul Shift™ Was Born

A brief synopsis of my life will help as I explain how Soul Shift™ was born.

My childhood was filled with all forms of abuse and neglect. My parents divorced when I was three. My father was given custody of us kids, and my mother just sort of disappeared from our lives—with an occasional visit now and then. My new stepmother quickly became a closet alcoholic; she was as abusive as my father. I experienced significant abuse in this household—physical, emotional, sexual, and spiritual—at the hands of my father and stepmother. I was singled out from my siblings for special negative attention because my father often remarked I reminded him of my mother.

In our close-knit little town, everybody knew everybody and gossip spread easily and quickly. Everybody thought they knew everybody else's business, and if they didn't they were happy to make something up. The community had its own set of taboos and rules. Things like abuse and alcoholism were never mentioned. When strangers moved in, the whole town would whisper about the way the wife or children were treated, or the amount the father drank, but the idea that any of the stalwart members of the community would behave in such a manner was unthinkable.

I tried to tell people what was going on in my home, but I was accused of being a liar and a troublemaker. Eventually, I stopped trying to tell anyone.

Once a boy—I'll call him Tyler—moved into town with his father. They lived in a camper on the back of their truck. All of the girls in my grade, including me, were smitten by this handsome new boy. When my father found out I liked Tyler, he proceeded to tell me what a terribly lazy, filthy, drunken thief Tyler's father was. According to my father, Tyler was guilty by association and would certainly grow to be just as bad as his father. I can still hear the tone in my father's voice as he described in detail every perceived fault Tyler's dad possessed.

The next day, as I listened to one of the girls in my class describe how much she liked Tyler, I felt it was my duty to repeat everything my father had told me in exactly the same tone of voice, so she would know what a bad choice she was making. She looked at me in amazement and quietly said, "You don't know that's true. Besides, I'm not interested in his father. I'm interested in Tyler, and I know he is a good, kind person."

All these years later, I have never forgotten this lesson given by my classmate. Do not judge others, do not gossip, and do not believe everything you're told.

Tyler and his father moved after only a few short months in our town, and I often wondered if it was because of the social pressure of poisonous tongues wagging.

Just before my 15th birthday, my father tried to have me placed in the foster care system. Professionals intervened, circumstances changed, and I was finally able to move to another state and live with my mother. Mom provided shelter and food, but little else. However, I did feel the love and support of my dear grandparents, who lived nearby. The relief I felt at no longer living in my father's household was palpable, but I tiptoed around my mother, fearful that I would make a mistake and she would send me back again. While I was no longer being physically or sexually abused, the repercussions of the abuse I had suffered as a child tainted and colored my world.

Over the next four years, I made mistakes—stupid, painful choices that I now know could be mapped as the normal course of events by an expert in the field of adult survivors of child abuse.

By the time I was 20, I was an unhappy wife and mother. I began to have terrifying feelings of rage, and I fought powerful urges to treat my darling child the way I had been treated. I sought professional help and came to understand the map an abused person often follows. I understood the reasons for my choices and why I felt the way I did. I began to understand it was okay to insist on safety for myself, and that I needed to provide a safe environment for my daughter. With those new understandings, it became necessary to divorce my first husband and try to start again.

My second marriage was not much better than the first. The reason, of course, was I took myself with me into the second marriage. I had not addressed or dealt with some of my unhealthy core issues. While I understood myself on an intellectual level, the choices I made were still being dictated by my damaged soul.

Once again, I sought professional help. This time, I was given antidepressants along with talk therapy.

I hardly ever remember my dreams. If I do remember them, it only lasts for a few hours. However, I still remember vividly the dream I was having when I nearly strangled my husband while under the influence of an antidepressant.

I dreamed I was in a room with my father and stepmother. They were yelling and threatening me. My father was removing his thick leather belt in preparation to beat me, as he had many times when I was a child. In my dream it was different, though. I was an adult trained in martial arts, confident I could defend myself. Everything felt so real. I disabled my stepmother and then went after my father. I remember the pleasure and power I felt at wrapping my hands around my father's neck and squeezing. I could feel the warmth of his skin under my hands. I was determined that he would never hurt me again. Gradually, I became aware that someone was shaking me and calling my name. As I awoke and returned to consciousness, I discovered my hands were around my husband's throat and I was squeezing as hard as I could. I jerked my hands away from him. Amazingly, even as he was drawing in huge, gasping breaths, he was trying to comfort me. Horrified, I wondered what might have happened if I had dreamed I was stabbing my father with a knife. Would I have killed my husband, or perhaps my children?

After that nightmare experience, I demanded to be weaned off the antidepressants.

Although many things changed because of my time in therapy, eventually after 12 years of marriage, I found it necessary to divorce husband number two. He had some issues he needed to deal with, and he was apparently not able to do so within the confines of our relationship. I decided it was better to be alone than to trust myself to make an intelligent choice regarding someone to spend my life with.

With this in mind, I occasionally dated but never allowed anyone to get really close. I was content with raising my three children on my own.

Enter my daughter's sixth grade teacher. I had only previously seen him from a distance. At our first parent-teacher conference, I was unprepared for and overwhelmed by the emotional connection I felt toward Mr. Jeffrey Nagel.

I tried to talk myself out of the feeling, telling myself that he was younger than I was, and what could he possibly see in a divorced mother of three children? Besides, I was *not* going to get involved with anyone ever again. Nevertheless, a year later we were married—but guess what? I had taken myself with me into yet another relationship.

Even though I had gone through therapy twice, I still had many of the same problems and feelings. My experience with talk therapy is that you drag all your negative memories and emotions into your lap, embrace them, and then at the end of your session, what do you do with them? They are still there, but now they are fresh in your mind ready to control you just like they did the day they originally happened. Talk therapy helped me identify my core issues but provided no truly effective tools to help resolve them.

I had been actively involved in self-help therapies for many years before marrying Jeffrey, so one of the things that attracted me to him was that he, too, was interested in improving himself. He was interested in making our relationship the best it could be, and he knew this involved making some changes in his own life.

The name "Soul Shift" came about as a result of a rather noisy conversation we were having one lovely summer morning in Arizona. I was trying to explain to him how I wanted to write a book and create a healing resort, where I could teach the things I have learned over the years about shifting out of your past and becoming who you really want to be.

There are plenty of strange concepts out there in the world, and I was going through the process of combining the essential elements of what I had learned into a structure for a program. Perhaps my greatest gift is my intuition, and I knew intuitively that bringing together selected pieces from all that I had learned into a new system would create a unique and deeply powerful method to help people heal emotionally and spiritually. I knew the program I needed to create would address all aspects of a person—their physical, emotional, intellectual, and spiritual selves—in order to enable them to heal on all levels. My personal healing would not have been accomplished without the power of my relationship with the Savior.

Frustrated because I could not make him understand what I was trying to accomplish by my studies, I struggled to put my vision into words that he *could* understand.

Pretend you are a fly on the wall watching a portion of our conversation.

"I don't understand what you are trying to accomplish," he exclaimed. "I see you studying all these different things that seem so disjointed and make no sense to me, and I wonder what happened to your faith? What happened to the woman I married who was so grounded?"

"You're right. You don't understand," I agreed. "I believe that people who are in the deepest pain are not truly able to connect with God. They cannot see past the pain of their own darkness long enough to really look up, let alone trust Him. If man is created in God's image, and all the men they've ever known are abusive, how can they take the chance of trusting God? I want to help people get rid of the pain that keeps them separate from God.

"They can go through therapy, take drugs, read a ton of books, and study all sorts of alternative healing, but all the garbage is still there. Deep in their souls, they are still controlled by the past and by the negative way they feel about themselves. I want to teach other people how to get rid of all that garbage completely. They need to release it from their core, get it out of their cells, out of the deepest part of themselves. I want to teach people how to . . . to . . . soul shift!"

At this point, his jaw dropped and his eyes lit up. He got so excited, he went to the white board where he puts all his thoughts and designed a Soul Shift™ logo for me right on the spot. We started bubbling over with ideas and thoughts, and what had started as a difficult conversation transformed into a session of brilliant, life-giving, enthusiastic brainstorming. The core ideas of Soul Shift™ emerged from this conversation, and they have continued to be shaped by my work with clients.

## What is Soul Shift™?

In a quiet reflective moment, have you ever wondered how you got to where you are today? This can either be a good thing or a bad thing, but most often when we have these moments they occur because we are in pain and we are not happy with the direction our lives have taken.

Somehow, the dreams we originally envisioned have not materialized and we feel terribly unhappy. Maybe we feel guilty because we are not satisfied with what we have, or maybe our lives are just so painful we want to give up trying to make positive changes and curl up in a dark corner somewhere to hide.

There are three paths someone who is suffering can take: destruction, denial, or ascent—rising above the pain. Many people turn to self-destructive choices (alcohol, drugs, or other addictions) to numb the pain. Others deny there is a problem and live in quiet desperation. The truly brave believe there is something better, and they seek help to make the positive changes their soul hungers for.

Most of us have gone through this scenario. We have something we want to change. We want to be happier. Perhaps it is just that we want to think more positive thoughts. We know that Proverbs 23:7 says, "As he thinketh in his heart, so is he."

Much of what we have heard or read about in self-help books tells us that we need to make a conscious effort to control our thoughts. Whenever we find ourselves thinking a negative thought, we need to consciously replace it with a positive thought. So far, so good.

We go along in this vein for a while until we discover it really isn't easy to think positive thoughts about ourselves because we don't believe them, anyway. The little snarky voice in the back of our heads says something nasty, even as we are trying to say something nice about ourselves.

For some reason, we can hear the nasty little voice more clearly than the nice thoughts we consciously think. Eventually, we begin to sabotage ourselves again, which somehow only proves to us that the whole concept of "as a man thinketh" is nonsense because it did not work for us.

Our failure also seems to reaffirm that we are not worthy of whatever happiness or goal we think we want. For most people, changing habitual thought processes requires a gargantuan effort of sheer will, as well as time.

There are some people who are able to make immediate changes in their way of thinking by exerting such a monumental force of will that it is surprising the mountains do not fall down. I am in awe of these people; however, most of us have to put in a little bit more work in order to achieve change.

## What is Trauma?

We often think of trauma as coming from some sort of physical, sexual, emotional, or intellectual abuse. Medical personnel refer to a serious accident or surgery as "trauma." But it could also be a betrayal of any kind. In reality, trauma can be experienced when anything happens in your life that rattles your perception of how things should be or how you believe they have always been. Trauma affects your psyche so much that you are no longer able to look at life in the same way because you feel that everything you believed to be true has been proven to be false. It can be anything that affects you on a deeply profound level. If the experience shakes you to your very core and strips away your feeling that you are safe in the world, it is rightly labeled "trauma."

We don't usually think of a difficult birth as being traumatic, or perhaps a medical test endured by a young child. After all, children are so resilient we tend to dismiss their experience. On a conscious level, the child might not ever be aware that the trauma took place, but the effects are long-lasting and they can definitely affect the child's view of life, as well as their unconscious behavior.

When you experience something terrible, your entire self participates in the experience. You are completely there—emotions, mind, body, and spirit—and every single part of you resonates with the terrible experience. The trauma is not just an isolated, intellectual event. This is why just talking about trauma or drugging the memory into submission is often ineffective in helping a person achieve true and lasting healing.

## Engaging Your Mind, Body, and Soul

The most powerful healing methods engage every single part of you, just as the negative experience did. However, most of us have never been given the tools, blueprint, or instruction on how to achieve our desired transformation.

On a long drive many years ago, my youngest daughter was riding in the back seat with her sister. I was riding in the passenger seat, and (as I always did) I looked back to check on how the kids were doing. I knew the drive was tedious for little people trapped in car seats. As usual, she had undone her car seat buckles and was free.

When I saw she had escaped again, I was exasperated because she was quite good at undoing the buckles, but she had not figured out how to do them back up again. It was a game she liked to play that drove me to distraction.

I turned around in my seat, took the buckles in my hands, and said, "You have to have your buckles done up."

Immediately, she threw a fit, pushing my hands away and yelling, "No, mommy! Me do! Me do!"

I took my hands away and said, "Alright, fine. Do it yourself."

Less than two seconds later, she tearfully wailed, "I can't!"

Do you ever feel this way when all you want is to make a change and do things differently? You really want to do it, but you do not feel like you can. You don't have the slightest idea where to start. You do not have the tools necessary to make the change. Even though you have read a great self-help book that inspired you for a moment, you do not know how to make the shift in your soul that indicates real change.

Perhaps you don't really know what you want. You just know that what you have right now is *not* it.

Many people misunderstand the quest to know themselves. We are not supposed to be selfish, self-absorbed, or self-centered. We are supposed to serve others and be selfless, but our journey through life is really quite individual. We are born individually and die the same way. Our relationship to our Savior is also unique. Our Heavenly Father views us as individuals, and our experiences are all our own.

You and I could witness the exact same accident and have two very different memories and impressions about what happened. We could have been raised in the same home and still have different experiences and opinions arising from the same kind of treatment. Twins can ride in the same rollercoaster car and have drastically different experiences on the ride.

I cannot make it back to Heavenly Father's presence on borrowed faith or someone else's prayers. I require an individual relationship with Him. Our recovery from the horrid experiences we have had is also our own.

What we make of our lives is individual, but we cannot do it without the help of others. Most importantly, we cannot return to dwell with God without the help of the Savior, Jesus Christ.

It is interesting to see how intricately we are interwoven with each other, and yet how separate we are at the same time.

In my personal journey towards a Soul Shift, I constantly sought the next best thing that would help me reach my goals. I went through some amazing programs, which I am absolutely convinced would have worked but for my basic problem. I believed my circumstances had always been bad and they always would be bad. Deep down, I believed I did not deserve to be happy and I was not worthy of a good life. I had to let go of this limiting belief in order to allow my Soul Shift to take place.

Although we are talking about childhood issues and events that occurred while we were living in our houses of origin, Soul Shift™ is not about placing blame or being disrespectful of our families. It is about healing ourselves and connecting with God or our higher power in a deeper, more fulfilling manner.

As adults, we are accountable for how we conduct ourselves every moment of every day.

Soul Shift™ is about healing our past wounds so we can have a more fulfilling, joyful present and future. It's a feeling of something inside of us suddenly coming into perfect alignment and we finally understand how our lives have been out of balance. Soul Shift brings us firmly into contact and awareness of our true nature, just as God intended. Before the Shift, our gears were out of synch, but afterwards they will finally be connected properly.

You cannot successfully have a Soul Shift by yourself. You must include the Savior or whoever is your higher power. This is an immutable and eternal law, and sometimes you must accept help from gifted professionals who can teach you new tools for healing.

Look at it this way: It is not normal to intentionally move toward pain. Our bodies and minds are programmed to avoid pain and danger whenever possible. It is a natural survival instinct. When we are working on the most painful parts of ourselves, our minds will tend to slide sideways in order to protect us by directing us away from the painful memory, trauma, or unwanted behavior.

When you have an intuitive guide you trust, this person can help you move past the blocks and bypass the safety mechanisms you have employed to protect yourself without compromising your sense of safety.

When I run my seminars and workshops with a group of people who have come for healing and transformation, the power we create together and the safety we feel in our little community helps us move from being stuck and in pain to finding hope and choosing joy.

## Three Important Rules for Soul Shift™

- Let Go Of Blame. Although someone else's choices or behavior might have caused the traumas we experienced, or they might have trained us in the way we currently feel about ourselves, we are responsible for our own responses and behavior from this point on. Forgiveness is essential to Soul Shift; however, forgiveness is a process that usually takes time and work. When we work through the pain, forgiveness is not only possible, but it is a natural side effect of Soul Shift™.

- Soul Shift™ Is An Individual Process. We are so habituated to comparing ourselves to others that it might be hard at first *not* to compare our progress using Soul Shift™ to others. Someone else might have a drastic and immediate life-altering shift. If you compare yourself to another person's progress, you might miss the milestones in your own progress, especially if your milestones initially seem smaller.
- Treat Yourself Kindly. Acknowledge the growth you are making and love yourself without conditions. Unconditional love creates an atmosphere in which the soul can expand. When we are free of fear, we can see more clearly—new avenues of action will open up and new choices will appear.

So many people seek to change themselves and others by negative means. We cajole, we bribe, we criticize and condemn, manipulate, and control. None of these behaviors will result in permanent change for the better. In fact, they can create an atmosphere of fear, which limits rather than encourages growth.

There is also a health aspect to Soul Shifting. Our bodies and minds must be nourished. It is necessary to eat mindfully. Practice eating consciously, being aware of everything you put in your mouth. Accepting responsibility for your choices means learning to eat only as much as your body needs and paying attention to *what* you eat. Remember, your soul is your spirit and your body together as one. Processed foods often contain all sorts of chemicals that mess with your brain and body chemistry, which can cause your mood and emotions to become imbalanced and your body to stop functioning properly. It is hard to heal when you put a lot of junk into your body.

CHAPTER FOUR

# The Wall
*Why We Do the Things We Do*

**Definition of Authority:** "(a) The power or right to give commands, enforce obedience, take action or make final decisions; jurisdiction; (b) the position of one having such power, a person in authority."

—yourdictionary.com

## The Wall

There is a *wall* inside of every innocent child who comes to live on earth. This wall is an absolutely pristine, blank slate on which our lessons and experiences are recorded for future reference. Our internal programming takes place on our wall.

While we are growing up, people who are important to us are deeply chiseling *their* values and *their* expectations for us on this wall. These people are our *authorities*. We instinctively look to them for safety and protection—whether they provide it or not is another thing, altogether. Our authorities can be parents, grandparents, older or more powerful siblings, peers we look up to, teachers, coaches, religious leaders, people in the foster care system, or anyone else who holds authority over us.

Every time we are presented with an idea, new or not, we hold it up against the wall to see if it lines up with what is inscribed there. If it does not, we reject it, even if it is something we really want to believe or do in our heart of hearts. The information on our wall is so deeply etched that to go against it challenges our very being. These etchings are the scripts that govern our lives.

It is scary and painful to challenge the writing on our wall. When we try to change, ignore, or go against what our authorities have written, the guilt or fear of being disobedient causes all sorts of conflict in our souls. The writings on your wall become your belief system. They are the standards against which you compare everything.

Can you remember, as a child, deliberately defying your mother or father? You grew by pushing boundaries and determining what you could and couldn't get away with. You knew some punishment would be meted out if you did something your parents didn't approve of, but sometimes you did it anyway. When the punishment was administered, it was engraved on your wall, too, especially if it was out of proportion to the mischief. Regardless of how many years you are past childhood, the imagined fear of punishment will often stop you in your tracks if you defy the writings on your wall. At the very least, it will cause you grave discomfort.

If someone tells you that you are beautiful, and it's not what you have been told all your life, you will not believe it no matter how true it is. If you were abused by your authorities, who engraved, "You are worthless" on your wall, and later someone tries to tell you that you are a precious, priceless child of God, you will not believe this either.

Some of the impressions engraved on your wall might not serve you when you are an adult. They can grow and become stumbling blocks to your progress, barriers to your dreams, and cruel taskmasters determined to maintain the status quo of your life. Our comfort zones are engraved on our inner walls.

Most likely, you can still hear the voices of your authorities telling you what is safe and what is not. As a child, you might have been told: "You cannot cross the street by yourself." When you become an adult, this can translate into fear of looking for a new job. After all, if you do not have the skills necessary to cross the street by yourself, how can you do something scary like look for a new job? The fear of stepping outside of your comfort zone can paralyze you.

Perhaps you can still hear your siblings taunting you when you tried to do something new. "Sarah is a dummy" (insert your name) chanted in a singsong voice can translate into an inability as an adult to make decisions because you fear making a mistake.

You might never forget the cruel voices of your peers at school chanting, "Fatty, fatty, two by four . . . ," in spite of the fact that you were an average-sized kid. The humiliation you felt then is just as powerful now that you are an adult, as you struggle to maintain a healthy weight or believe that your current weight is healthy and acceptable.

In your memory, you can clearly bring up the exact tone of ridicule your teacher used to humiliate you in public because of a mistake you made on the chalkboard while solving a fourth grade math problem. "How can you be so dumb?" said to you as a child might translate as an adult to, "I am not smart enough to become a scientist or start my own business."

You still feel deep shame because when you were a child your parents implied or said you were stupid. "You don't have enough brains to come in out of the rain" might now translate into constantly doubting your own abilities, no matter what you try to accomplish.

Some beliefs are inscribed deeply on your wall; others are merely scratched on the surface. How important the authority was to you when you were a child will determine how deeply their programming was etched on your wall.

For example, being verbally rejected by that cute boy or girl you were completely smitten with in fourth grade is likely to have been engraved quite deeply. On the other hand, the grouchy old lady down the street who called you a troublemaker might not have made much of a dent unless she reinforced the engravings your beloved Uncle Johnny had already etched on your wall.

In addition to how you feel about yourself, the engravings on your wall dictate how you are likely to feel about other things. Your current relationship with money, for example, was most likely engraved on your wall by those who raised you. The way you feel about God, the way you look at other people, what kind of food is acceptable for dinner, and what kinds of clothes you should wear were all programmed into your psyche.

You go through your day checking every decision, new idea, or feeling that comes your way against the engravings that rule your life. After comparing, you make your choices based on these beliefs. Just like breathing, it goes on automatically without you even being aware of it.

Are you beginning to get an idea of how crucial it is for people to be mindful and kind in their roles as parents, siblings, teachers, and friends?

## The Poverty of Low Expectations

How you live and the level of prosperity you achieve is directly related to the level of expectations your authorities held for you.

If you were raised in poverty, and it is all you and everyone in your family lineage has ever known poverty is likely to be what is expected for you—to remain poor because that's just the way it is. Changing the status quo and breaking out of poverty will not be easy, nor will it be supported by your relatives and peers, who will accuse you of trying to be better than they are. Many people who escape poverty feel guilty and ashamed because they aren't meeting the expectations on their wall.

The expectation that a child will follow in the footsteps of previous generations and take up the family business is deeply ingrained in many cultures. For example, if many of your family members have been lawyers or been in the military for generations, the expectation is that you will also be a lawyer or join the military. The pressure stemming from these kinds of expectations is huge, should you decide that you want to do something different with your life. Maybe you want to be an actor or an airline stewardess. You can actually become ill as a result of the internal conflict raging inside of you as you try to exert your own will against these authorities.

For centuries there have been social classes, and heaven help anyone who tried to move out of their designated class. The offender often experienced violence coming from both sides—the class they were trying to leave and the class they were trying to enter.

Many of the engravings on our walls can be debilitating, but some are worse than others. If the authorities on our walls told us that we are worthless, we are never going to amount to anything, and we are losers, it will be quite difficult for us to achieve success and happiness as adults. This type of belief can become the very core of who we are and how we see ourselves.

## Our Perceptions

It is easy to assume that the people who raised us were trying intentionally to belittle or shame us. However, they might have actually been trying to teach us what they felt were important life lessons. It helps if you can adopt the attitude that people are always doing the best they can with the limited tools at their command. Please understand, of course, that there are always exceptions to the rule. Some of our authorities were not very nice to us deliberately; this is discussed further in Chapter Four.

Our perception of a life lesson is not always what our authorities are attempting to teach us. As an example, my youngest son, Jeffrey Junior, attended one of Jack Canfield's *Break Through to Success* seminars with my husband and me when he was 16.

Several of his beliefs were challenged during the weeklong seminar. At the end of the second day, Jeffrey was furious with his father. He was so angry that he was fighting back tears, and he could not even stand to be in the same room with his dad. Fortunately, he was able to talk with me about what was going on.

Jeffrey felt that his dad had taught him several limiting beliefs, and he was furious. How could his dad do such a thing? Shouldn't a parent build a child up? However, the things he had heard his dad tell him were not at all what his dad had said.

There's an old saying in my family that illustrates this perfectly. It goes like this: *I know you think you understand what it is you thought I said, but I'm not sure you understand that what you heard is not what I meant.*

It took many long hours, but we were able to work through some of the misunderstandings. His dad was able to explain what he had intended to teach Jeffrey, and Jeffrey was able to explain what he had actually heard. They went out to the hotel's hot tub and spent time talking and rebuilding their relationship until the wee hours of the morning.

The next day in the course of the seminar, more beliefs were challenged. At the end of the day, I asked Jeffrey how he was doing. He snarled something in response, and I said, "Oh, it's my turn now, is it?" We had to work through some stuff, too.

Through this experience, my husband and I discovered that although we had absolutely no intention of giving our children limiting beliefs, the perception that our children took away from the lessons was not always what we had intended to teach them.

When Jeffrey Junior was about 12, our neighbor invited him to help him practice roping a calf. The "calf" was a metal shape attached to the back of an ATV. Jeffrey's job was to drive the ATV around a circular area while our neighbor rode behind on his horse and tried to rope the metal calf.

They did this for about two hours. Afterwards, our neighbor gave Jeffrey $50. What did I do? I thought $50 was a bit unreasonable for driving an ATV for a couple of hours.

In the first place, Jeffrey had never driven one before, and he was hoping I would give him permission to do it. In my opinion, it was not a "job" he should be paid for—he was playing. In the second place, how difficult is it to drive around in circles? He admitted to me that after the first 30 minutes, it got kind of boring.

My final bit of reasoning was that I wanted him to understand the value of money and get a better perspective between the value of work and payment for his work.

In the light of what I know now, I shudder when I remember thinking this way. My belief system dictated that you had to work a certain number of hours in order to get a certain amount of pay, and that the amount of money the neighbor had given Jeffrey was way out of proportion to the amount of "work" he had done.

I asked him to give half the money back to the neighbor, which he did. The neighbor, who was quite a successful and wealthy man, was dismayed that Jeffrey was required to return half the money. He had, after all, paid Jeffrey what *he* felt the job was worth.

As my son shared his frustration with me in the seminar, I thought back to this incident. As I checked the events against my belief wall, I realized that I had responded to my son based on the words deeply inscribed by my authorities:

"You must work hard for your money; it doesn't grow on trees."
"Rich people are crooks. How do you think they got so rich?"
"Never take money from strangers."
"You only get paid what the job is worth."

I have since grown out of this mindset, but at the time it was the best I could do. It was what I had been taught, and I thought it was what a good mom should teach her child. However, the lesson Jeffrey took away from our interaction was not what I had intended. He said he thought I did not believe he was good enough to make that kind of money and that he didn't deserve to make lots of money.

What I was trying to teach him and what he perceived from my words and actions were completely different. He carried this belief around with him for four years before he talked about it with me. Fortunately, we were able to work through this tragic bit of accidental programming, but many people don't get this opportunity while they are still young. As a result, they carry limiting beliefs around for decades.

How do our perceptions affect what we believe someone is saying to us? It depends on how we perceive the person, whether they are an authority, or how much value we place on the relationship, but it can have some very powerful side effects.

A tip: Do not argue with other people about their perceptions. They are speaking about their personal realities. They are the only ones who can do this. If you can step back and give up your need to be right and really listen to what the other person is saying, then rapport between you will be strengthened and you might be able to work through the miscommunication.

## Emotions

I have four very nearly perfect children. I love each of them with all of my heart. In the process of raising them, I have always tried to be absolutely fair with each one of them. I have tried to be consistent in the way I raised them, and I have tried to give each one my very best.

However, even though I tried to raise all my children in exactly the same way, each of them had a different experience growing up. This is because they are individuals, not little clones of each other, or of their parents, for that matter. They might have some characteristics in common. By looking at them, you can tell they are siblings, but they have individual personalities and they responded to my parenting efforts quite differently.

Because I was raised in a home where people screamed at each other and called each other horrid names, I made a conscious choice not to yell at my children or allow them to yell at each other.

The rule was: "You are allowed to yell at me if the house is on fire or if you are bleeding to death, but other than this, you must be respectful when you speak to me. You can say whatever you need to say no matter how awful it is, but it must be done in a respectful tone of voice."

Even though I never yelled at my children, they sometimes felt like they were being yelled at. I could use the same tone of voice with two different children who had participated in some mischief together, and one would take it in stride but the other would be convinced I was yelling. Once I had to demonstrate the difference between speaking sternly and yelling to one of my poor children so he would understand the difference. As the color drained from his face, he understood the nuances immediately. This was the only time I ever yelled at one of my kids.

Even if we grow up in the same house with a whole bunch of other people, our experiences will not be the same. We will be marked in a different way because our perspective is uniquely ours. Even in the most loving household, nobody makes it through childhood without some sort of battle scars. Firstborn children are the unwitting guinea pigs as their inexperienced parents try to figure out how to raise the completely dependent little person. Children get "dethroned" as new siblings show up, and parents change as well—either intentionally for the better, or digressing as a result of their own defective childhood or traumatic life circumstances.

Children growing up in an abusive environment remember their experiences differently, too. If you grew up in an abusive home, chances are your siblings—if you had any—remember things differently than you do. Perhaps they do not remember the abuse at all, locking it away in their subconscious as a way of protecting themselves so they can cope with the world.

One sibling might have chosen an addiction to help him (or her) cope, while the other acts as though nothing happened and wonders why the first sibling is such a loser. Yet other siblings might have escaped the abuse because their parents really did treat them differently. Perhaps the parents had changed because of a Soul Shift of their own, and their former parenting methods were no longer acceptable to them.

I know each of my children had a "different" mother, as I consciously worked on improving my skills and getting rid of old baggage from my own childhood.

When you listen to your siblings talk about their memories of growing up, do you ever say to yourself, *What on earth are you talking about? Did we even live in the same house? Did we have the same parents?*

Many years ago, I worked for an insurance company typing up accident reports. Frequently, I would be listening to a tape and stop typing in astonishment as the eyewitnesses each gave a completely different account of what was supposed to have been the same accident.

You can have ten people at the same scene, but you will get ten completely different narratives of what "really" happened. Although these ten people might have actually been there, they each had a different perspective or a different agenda, as in the case of one driver who was drunk. His report told of an entirely different person driving the car!

Our perspectives are based on many different factors, including birth order, personality, the way we were raised, whether we felt we had enough or that we were in want, our personal experiences, our culture, our beliefs, and our expectations, just to name a few.

Do you ever wonder how two children raised in the same circumstances can be so completely different? One might be miserably unhappy, spreading that unhappiness everywhere he (or she) goes, but the other is happy, generous, and smiling all the time.

The authorities who raised you decided which emotions you were allowed to show or not show, and they inscribed those instructions on your wall. Negative emotions, in particular, are not acceptable in many households.

I have a client, Cheryl, who was never allowed to show anger because it was not considered a "good" emotion in her home. She learned that rather than dealing with her anger, everyone should pretend it wasn't there. Falsely bright smiles, overly polite tones of voice, and clenched teeth were not enough to mask the angry vibrations emanating from whoever was upset. Cheryl's grandmother, who was a very angry woman, died of cancer of the bowel. Some scientists believe there is a link between repressive personalities and cancer.

In John's home, boys weren't allowed to be afraid—only sissies showed fear. He was called names like "scaredy-cat" or "fraidy-cat," and he was publicly ridiculed if he showed any kind of fear. Sometimes, when it came to doing something he felt was dangerous, his parents would mock him or force him to do whatever it was. A childhood like John's can leave tremendous battle scars.

Eric's sister was a constant thorn in his side. Although he was the elder sibling, she continuously got away with doing awful things to him because she was a girl. He remembers telling his mother, "I hate her!" His mother, with towering disapproval, said, "No you don't! You don't feel that way." Every time he expressed a negative emotion such as anger, his mother would say, "No, you don't feel that way."

As an adult, Eric still struggles with honestly recognizing his own emotions and accurately identifying them.

Emotions are chemicals released in response to our interpretation of a specific trigger. These chemicals are released throughout the body, forming a feedback loop between the brain and body. Our emotions are doing their job to keep us safe, help us to reproduce, interpret, and give us feedback about our environment. When an emotion is triggered, it travels throughout the body waiting to be noticed by us and validated; or in other words, owned and acknowledged. Once it is validated and acknowledged, the emotion is processed, causing no harm to the body or mind. But when an emotion is not processed, the emotional energy can become stuck in the body. It becomes a tangled ball of energy that lodges in our weakest organs and cells, and illness begins.

Think of emotions as if they are little children. They come to us for approval and say, *Look at me, I am happy,* or *pay attention to me; I am so angry* or *help me, I am frightened.* If you spend a moment to acknowledge your emotions and express them they will not cause problems. However, if you do not acknowledge your emotions, either by yourself or with someone you trust, you can get stuck in a loop. The emotion will rear its head again at some point in your life when it is triggered by another stimulus similar to the first one, which you ignored.

When you stuff your emotions, they get buried deep down inside your body at the cellular level. This is a defense mechanism your mind uses to protect you so you don't have to deal with the emotion or trauma—especially if you don't have the strength or support to face it. Unfortunately, if you don't deal with your suppressed emotions, they will constantly bubble up to the surface and affect your day-to-day life. Random flavors, odors, and tiny, seemingly inconsequential incidents can trigger a memory you've stored, and your panicked mind will respond with a knee-jerk reaction that can get you into all sorts of trouble.

If you have gone through a particularly traumatic incident and you are able to immediately tell somebody about it, and they are supportive and validating, you can say, "That was a horrible experience. I learned something from it, and I will never let anything like that happen to me again." The emotion can then be processed. Timing is very important in this. If you stuff your emotions and then wait weeks or years to talk about the trauma with a supportive friend or therapist, it will be much more difficult to release the traumatic experience because it has been trapped at the cellular level.

However, if you did try to tell somebody and they insisted the trauma or event did not happen or that you are out of your mind, the emotions surrounding it will not get processed. If they shame you by insisting the trauma is your fault, they are actually heaping additional trauma on the top of the first. People who are unable to discuss their trauma because it was caused by their parents—normally the person in whom a child would confide—also experience an intensification of the trauma. The same is true of people who feel they cannot tell what happened because of shame—rape or incest victims, for example, and people who were sexually molested by a priest or teacher.

I know an elderly woman I'll call Iris. When she was just a young girl of 14, she was babysitting a neighbor's child. There was a knock on the door. She opened it, and discovered a man standing there. When he determined there was no one else in the home except a baby, he forced his way inside, brutally raped Iris, and then left.

The police were called. When they arrived, they were cold and hostile. Iris was subjected to medical examinations that were almost as traumatic as the first violation. Within hours, everyone in the small town knew of the rape. Iris was shunned, whispered about, and openly blamed. She was told the rape was her fault. She must have led the man on. She must have done *something* to encourage him. The police half-heartedly looked for the rapist, but once they discovered he was from out of town they dropped the case. Although this happened over 66 years ago, Iris has suffered terribly from the experience her entire life. Unfortunately, things haven't changed that much in the world. Women are still being accused of being the cause of crimes committed against them.

When your emotions are not validated, trauma cannot be released. It gets trapped and continuously runs through your body and your mind like a hamster stuck on a wheel. The next time something happens that triggers a particular memory or the events associated with it, you flinch.

If you experience another trauma and it also is not acknowledged, it gets stuffed down on top of the previous one, until you end up having all of these stuffed emotions in your body. They almost look like layers of an onion. At random and unexpected times, these layers can come loose and the memories pop up, controlling your life in ways you had not expected and that you do not like. Your mind has skillfully hidden the cause of the pain and most of the time you are not even aware of what is going on. You just know that sometimes your life is quite unbearable.

## 100% Responsibility

Life changes when you take 100% Responsibility for your choices and outcomes, meaning you no longer blame other people or events for the quality of your life. This includes your upbringing, your parents, church leaders, teachers, your boss, the weather, or the circumstances in which you live. When you stop complaining and understand that your *response* to the events in your life determines the outcome, everything changes. The only thing you can completely control is your response to whatever happens. When you make the conscious choice to accept 100% Responsibility for yourself, you will have discovered the most powerful and enlightening tool you can ever apply to bring about positive change.

Soon after learning this concept, I was complaining to my husband about a web designer who had not followed my instructions. I was going on and on and on, until I noticed his eyes glaze over. I stopped and asked, "Why am I talking to you about this? You can't do anything about it!"

Then I got on the phone and had a conversation with the only person who could do something about it: the web designer.

One of my clients has taken the concept of 100% Responsibility to her work force. She called to give me an update as to how her office staff was doing with the training I had given them. When she inquired about a task she said it was very interesting to hear them say, "Well, I couldn't do it because . . ." and then they would stop and say, "Wait a minute, I have to accept 100% Responsibility for it. I didn't get that task done because I chose to do something else instead."

She said the conversations around the workplace were absolutely changed and the work was being done much more efficiently and effectively.

Look at the difference between, "It makes me mad when you [do whatever]," versus "I choose to be mad when you [do whatever]." The first statement gives away all your power. The second statement keeps your power with you. You cannot *make* me mad. I can *choose* to respond with anger to what you do or say, but you cannot *make* me mad.

Negative statements that are not accepting 100% Responsibility would be:

"I can't help it. It's my parents' fault."
"I was born this way."
"This is just the way I am."

When you accept 100% Responsibility for your life, you affirm:

"I can help it."
"I am responsible for my choices from now on."

This change in your perspective and behavior can be incredibly powerful.

## Our Earliest Experiences

Nobody gets through life without a few emotional scars. The very best, most loving parents in the world will inevitably make some mistakes in parenting. I have always felt it's an oversight that babies come into the world without an owner's manual.

Wouldn't it be much easier if we knew what the inarticulate child was trying to tell us with their piercing screams? Eventually, an attentive parent will begin to understand the different nuances in the way the infant communicates, but there is a whole lot of trial and error involved. Then, just when the parents think they have finally figured out parenting, child number two comes along with a completely different set of needs and ways communicating, and the frazzled parent gets to start all over again.

One of the most valuable processes through which we learn is called "feedback." It can be positive or negative and sometimes even neutral, but our response to feedback is the way in which we learn to navigate our world.

From the moment of conception, we are given feedback from the people in the world around us. During pregnancy, the infant is intimately aware of its mother's emotions and thoughts. There is no shielding or hiding these thoughts from the infant, because he (or she) shares everything with the mother, including hormones, nutrients, and blood.

The Association for Prenatal and Perinatal Psychology and Health (APPPAH) says a baby's experience of conception, pregnancy, and birth creates lifelong consequences for individual families and society. This is has been validated by scientific studies.

In addition, the birth process itself is very difficult for babies as well as mothers. Few births are calm and gentle. Some of them are downright traumatic. Because birth is so commonplace, we tend to think only of the trauma of the mother, without realizing that the infant has also experienced an excruciating and painful entrance into the world.

In a hospital setting, bright lights sting eyes that are accustomed only to warm darkness. To add insult to injury, almost immediately after separation from our mother, we are poked with needles and prodded with cold instruments. Some of us were slapped, others had oxygen blown into our faces, and a few of us were dropped.

Those who came into the world surgically have their own set of traumas.

In our first moments of life, we are scrutinized to make sure all our fingers and toes are accounted for, examined in the hope that we have departed the womb meeting all the expectations of perfection carried in the minds of our parents and other family members.

While growing in the womb, however, no one bothered to tell us about the standard of expected perfection, and there was nothing we could do about it anyway.

The comments that go on over our heads tell us that we look like Aunt Mary or Grandpa George, or nobody in the family at all. Where did we get that nose, that chin, our tiny slanted eyes or prominent ears? Although the conversation was not directed at us, we nevertheless picked up on the "vibes."

If we were fortunate enough to have been a wanted child, greatly anticipated and loved, this was conveyed to us in the way we were cared for. We got feedback in caresses, loving words, affection, and tenderness, and our needs were responded to. The majority of the feedback we received was positive and nurturing, and we had a greater chance of feeling pretty good about ourselves as we grew up.

If, however, we were not wanted, or we were born into a home with parents who harbored their own wounds and were not emotionally able to care for us and love was in scant supply, the feedback was mostly negative. When our physical and emotional needs are not adequately met, the phrase "scarred for life" is extremely accurate.

## Clients Who Changed the Writing on Their Walls

There are many ways to release stuck beliefs that no longer serve you. The writing on your wall contains ideas, not unchangeable concrete facts of the universe. They can be changed.

There are many tools you can use to change the writing on your wall. The first important thing is to realize the writing is even there. Look back and think about some of the things people told you while you were growing up and see how they are affecting you as an adult.

I had a client, Chad, who had an addiction to pornography. I worked with him using Emotion Freedom Technique (EFT). Chad had gone through years of regular therapy and had been prescribed medication, but he was still struggling with his addiction. He would be clean for six weeks and think everything was okay, and then something would trigger in his life and he would dive right back into addiction.

At the point he came to see me, his wife was ready to take the children and leave. He was very concerned and frightened because he did not want this consequence. However, he simply could not control his desire for pornography. He felt that coming to see me was his last resort before his life imploded.

In one of our sessions using EFT, a memory surfaced of something that happened when he was three. It appeared to have absolutely nothing to do with the compulsion Chad felt when he first started viewing pornography. There was no logical sequencing, no logical trauma you could point to that said, "This is why you are addicted to pornography."

When the memory first surfaced, he was completely puzzled about what it had to do with anything. He was surprised he even remembered it. It seemed such a trifling thing. Although he did not understand the trigger himself, we tapped on the experience because it had shown up while we were doing the work. Chad said he actually felt something shift inside him, and his entire affect changed. He has been completely free of his addiction for five years, now, and he is an addiction counselor for others who struggle to overcome addiction to pornography.

I had another client who was having tremendous difficulty with health issues. Rachel had terrible problems with pain in her abdominal area. The pain was the most intense in the morning. She had gone to numerous doctors, who were not able to help her at all. She came to me and I used SHEN with her. As I directed the flow of *chi* through her body, she curled up in the fetal position and began shaking. It was the strangest thing to watch.

She was not able to control it—she tried. It was as though I was chasing something around her body that did not want to go away. When I would reposition my hands to move the energy through one part of her body that was in spasm, energy would shoot across to the opposite side of her body and cause that area to curl up.

Neither of us knew what was going on. I asked Rachel if she was comfortable, or whether she wanted me to stop what I was doing. She asked me to keep working, although sweat stood out on her forehead. I quietly kept with it, as she persevered and went with it, too.

After an hour, all of her shaking and muscle spasms had stopped and she was calm. She took a deep breath, opened her eyes, and said with wonder, "I just remembered what happened to me!"

She told me there was a three-week period of her life that she had no memory of whatsoever. She knew something terrible must have happened, because you don't just lose three weeks of your life. All she remembered was that she woke up in the hospital and then went home. She didn't know why she had been in the hospital; although there were wounds and scars she had no memory of receiving. Yet, as she sat there in my office, she was clearly able to recall and describe the three-week period and the days leading up to it. She had been in the hospital in intensive care because her ex-husband had attempted to murder her.

Before the SHEN session, she had no memory of this event, because in order to spare her sanity her mind had stuffed the memory deep into her cellular tissues. We were chasing around her body the cellular memory of the wounds and trauma her body had experienced when her ex-husband tried to kill her. All this trapped traumatic energy was finally released.

After the session, she said she felt better than she could remember feeling in years. The next morning after she woke up, she called me in tears, saying that she had continued to remember the events of that horrible experience all through the night, but she said it was okay because her body was letting go of the trauma. She believed a tremendous burden had been lifted, and she felt happier than she could remember being in a long time. The most exciting thing for her was that the pain in her abdomen, which had plagued her for 20 years, was completely gone.

People in Western cultures often mock energy therapies. In Eastern cultures, such as China, Japan, and India, energy therapies have been used successfully for thousands of years. Scientific studies are beginning to prove the validity of therapies many people already know and trust from personal experience.

Western and Eastern medicine use very different paradigms when seeking to understand the body and its systems. Both are perfectly valid, but one can look a little alien when viewed from the context of the other.

A great way to think of this is illustrated in the story of the blind men meeting an elephant for the first time. One blind man, touching a leg, said the elephant is like a tree. Another, touching the trunk, said an elephant is like a giant snake. And yet a third man, touching the ear, said an elephant is like a giant fan. All are correct, but only by exploring the entire elephant can you get the full, complete picture.

If you put an atom underneath an electron microscope, you will discover that inside the atom there is a smaller substance, and inside this there is an even smaller substance. When you go deeper into the cells, you will discover that all we are is energy. Even though you look solid on the outside, you are made up of countless little particles of energy. Thus, it is very possible to make changes in your body through energy therapies.

## Questions to Think About

> What kind of things do you remember being engraved on your wall?
> Do you believe money really is the root of all evil?
> Do you believe rich people are all crooks?
> Do you believe you should not make more money than your parents did?
> Do you believe you do not deserve to be happy?
> Look at what kind of work you are doing for a living. Are you doing what *you* want to do and what makes *you* happy, or are you doing what your authorities said you should do for a living?

CHAPTER FIVE

# Survivors of Abuse
*Insights to Better Understand Yourself*

**Definition of Abuse:** "Abuse is a repetitive pattern of behaviors to maintain power and control over an intimate partner. These are behaviors that physically harm, arouse fear, prevent a partner from doing what they wish or force them to behave in ways they do not want. Abuse includes the use of physical and sexual violence, threats and intimidation, emotional abuse and economic deprivations. Many of these different forms of abuse can be going on at any one time."

—thehotline.org

Abuse has no boundaries. There are no religions, communities, cultures, or countries that are exempt from this pernicious evil.

Many people who seem perfectly good and wonderful on the outside can be demons in their own homes. When and if the abuse comes to light, all the friends and neighbors are stunned because the perpetrator appeared to be such a good person in public.

Victims of abuse have a tendency to believe the abuse was their fault. Perhaps if they had not cried or broken something, or dropped something, or forgotten something, or burned dinner, or been too noisy or . . . whatever it was, the pattern of victims is to take on the blame.

Of course, the individual who commits the abuse is more than happy to heap all of the blame onto the victim: "I would not have to hit you if you had obeyed me the first time. I would not have to make you go hungry if you had done what I told you to do."

Just as there are many abusers, there are multitudes of ways of being abused. There are also many ways to survive. One method is to become an emotional vegetable, even though you are still alive and breathing. Another is to move through each day on hyper-alert, while hoping you can avoid a recurrence of the trauma you survived. Yes, you survived, but you did not have the tools necessary to make your life into something that brings you joy. The ideal way to survive abuse is to move past it—to process your emotions, reclaim your power and live on your own terms, free of fear.

## ACEs Test

In the years between 1995 and 1997, volunteers from the Kaiser Permanente Healthcare System answered questionnaires regarding obesity. Doctors looked for patterns and tried to understand the lifestyles, habits, and childhood experiences of their obese patients. The study rapidly blossomed into something else that greatly surprised the researchers and made these hardened professionals, who thought they had seen and heard it all, weep.

When they asked the obese patients a series of questions regarding their childhood, they sometimes got answers for which they had not planned. It started with an accidental question a tired doctor asked, "How old were you when you first had sex?" even though the question on the paper read, "How much did you weigh when you first had sex?" When the patient hung her head and whispered, "Four," the doctor was stunned. He asked the question again, wrong this time on purpose. He got the same answer, with the added whisper, "It was my daddy."

Since then, doctors have asked this question intentionally.

After compiling the answers from approximately 17,000 patients, the Keizer doctors discovered patterns and evidence that adverse childhood experiences often lead to certain types of negative health outcomes.

The Center for Disease Control took up the study and helped develop a survey from the results of the Keizer research that is now used in progressive schools and health facilities. It is called "The Adverse Childhood Experiences" study, or "ACEs."

Ten types of childhood trauma were measured in the ACE study. These particular childhood traumas were selected because they were mentioned as being the most common, and because they had been well studied individually in research literature.

The most important thing to remember is that the ACE score is meant as a guideline. If you experience other types of toxic stress over months or years, this would also count as adverse experiences, such as being held captive or sexually trafficked. This type of experience is not specifically mentioned in the ACEs score, but it certainly would count.

Without going into the entire study here, suffice it to say that there are people in the world who have high ACEs and people who do not have any at all. There is an ACEs test for females and an ACEs test for males. Please see the References section at the end of this book for more information.

## What the ACEs Score Means

The CDC's Adverse Childhood Experiences study uncovered a stunning correlation between childhood trauma and the chronic diseases people develop as adults, as well as social and emotional problems. This includes heart disease, lung cancer, female cancers, diabetes, and many autoimmune diseases, as well as depression, violence, and being a victim of violence and suicide.

The study's researchers came up with an ACE score to explain a person's risk for chronic disease. Think of it as a cholesterol score for childhood toxic stress. You get one point for each type of trauma. The higher your ACE score, the higher your risk of health and social problems.

There are many are other types of trauma that can contribute to childhood toxic stress, including homelessness, being a refugee, being bullied, watching a sibling be abused by a parent, and loss of a caregiver other than your mother or father. Sibling abuse is not on the list, because there are few studies of this type of abuse. As you can imagine, it is possible that some people could have ACE scores higher than 10; however, the ACE study only measures up to 10.

As your ACE score increases, so does your risk of disease and social and emotional problems. With an ACE score of 4 or more, the possible repercussions of poor health as an adult increase exponentially. The likelihood of developing chronic pulmonary lung disease increases 390%, hepatitis increases 240%, depression increases 460%, and the likelihood of suicide increases 1,220%.

It is important to note that these studies were done with mostly white, middle or upper middle class, college-educated people with good jobs and good health care. The thought of all the people who don't match these demographics, and who are at greater risk for growing up in an abusive environment, makes this particular social epidemic terrifying to contemplate.

It can be difficult for people to admit these kinds of things have happened to them. Otherwise high-functioning adults will do anything to hide their adverse childhood experiences from others, and from themselves, because they often feel deep shame, certain that the abuse was their fault.

Catastrophic events happen every day that are nobody's fault. If someone is hurt in an earthquake, is it his (or her) fault? I witnessed the brakes go out on a bus on a steep street in San Francisco. It rolled backward and flattened a brand new Aston Martin. Thank goodness I had just watched the driver walk away moments earlier. Do you think the accident was the bus driver's fault? Was it perhaps the fault of the woman who parked her brand new car in that particular place? No, of course not.

Myriad emotions are involved when a person has had an adverse experience, regardless of the person's age. If I were bleeding, you would all rush to help me; however, the culture of the world does not rush to help those who are bleeding inside with unseen emotional wounds.

Again, emotions must be acknowledged. If you have a traumatic experience and you admit to yourself that it happened—and someone you trust validates your experience when you share it—then the emotion gets processed. If you do not have the opportunity to process an emotion, it will get stuck in your body and fester, creating health issues.

True healing requires a two-step process: self-validation, by admitting that the trauma happened to you, and validation from someone you trust.

When these two steps occur, the emotion gets processed and rarely causes any further problems. However, most of us are in the habit of stuffing our emotions and memories firmly into the deepest layer of our psyche, where they can create havoc with our well-being.

The ACEs study shows a definite link between female cancers and female sexual abuse. Unfortunately, sexual abuse is on the rise in the world, and yet those who have experienced it hide their heads in shame as though it was their fault—it was *not*.

Now is a good time to speak the truth about your life and your experiences. You do not have to shout your stories from the rooftops or allow them to spill over into the rest of your life. You don't have to tell anyone about what's happened to you if you don't want to, but you do have to face your experiences and be honest with yourself. Admit how your past experiences have shaped you and helped create your present circumstances.

Decide consciously to do some emotional house cleaning. Acknowledge your adverse childhood experiences. Take the test and see how the results make you feel. For me, it was an amazingly freeing experience to realize I wasn't crazy or broken.

Be honest about your relationships with your family and friends, both while you were growing up and now. Seek professional help, if necessary, to help root out any toxic emotions that are keeping you stuck and fearful of pursuing your dreams. One of my favorite quotes is by Anne Lamott, who wrote, "You own everything that happened to you. Tell your stories. If people wanted you to write warmly about them, they should have behaved better."

The truth is you are the person you are because of your experiences. You can either let them crush you, or you can fight to be who you *really are* and *who you want to be*. You can learn and grow and flourish, and then take your hard-earned knowledge and share it with the world. Your message is unique to you because of what you have lived through and overcome. The passion that drives you and the desire you have within you to make the world a better place are the result of the road you have traveled through life.

Wandering through the mall one day, I saw an amazing display titled *More Than A Survivor*. It was a photo display of women who had been sexually trafficked. They told their stories of how they entered into this life and how they escaped. I met Rebecca Bender, who was once sexually trafficked. She is very open about her experiences, and she is not afraid to talk about her difficult childhood, which led to her being trafficked. She understands and freely explains the reasons for her choice to willingly return to her pimp after breaking free. She is also unafraid to admit her strengths and talk about how she was finally able to leave that life completely. Her passion now is ministering to other women who are trying to break free. She also teaches law enforcement personnel how to recognize and help victims.

## The Difference between People with and without ACEs

The study goes on further to explain that there is a change in the brain structure of a child who has experienced toxic stress. The amygdala and hippocampus are smaller. The amygdala is associated with emotion and decision-making. The hippocampus is associated with emotional processing and memory formation. Cortisol, also called the "death hormone," is often present in higher concentrations in the bodies of people who have been abused. Thus, adult survivors of childhood abuse might legitimately have difficulty making decisions, processing their emotions, and remembering things.

The fight-or-flight area in the brain of a person who has experienced chronic, toxic stress does not respond to stimuli correctly because it has been stuck in the "on" position for years. It is one thing to see a bear in the woods and have an adrenaline rush that gives you the strength to get away from the bear, but another thing altogether when the bear lives with you and there is nowhere to hide or run to. Perhaps you are no longer in an abusive situation, but you still experience fight-or-flight reactions.

Do you jump when you hear a noise? Do you feel your skin crawl when you are walking to your car from a building and it is still sunny outside? Do you wake up in the middle of the night with your heart pounding because you thought you heard something out of the ordinary? Do you find yourself unable to sleep through the night?

Imagine that you have a high ACEs score and your partner has a low ACEs score. When you think they do not understand you, it is possible they really *don't* understand you because they have never experienced what you have experienced.

My husband has an ACEs score of perhaps 1. My ACEs score is 9. When I discovered the ACEs test, it gave me such incredible freedom because now I really get that when I say, "You don't understand," it is because he really *does not* understand. He has no point of reference. It is not a failing on his part. We just grew up in two very different worlds.

My husband had a safe childhood, so he does not understand my constant hyper-vigilance. Sometimes when we have disagreements, I might respond way out of proportion to the topic because something intangible in the confrontation has triggered my sense of not being safe.

Have your intimate partner take the ACEs test, too. It might help you level the playing field so you can both understand, *Ah, this is my ACEs score; this is his (or her) ACEs score; so there really is a difference in the way we think.*

## Unconscious Behaviors

People who have been abused often move around a lot, searching for something, although they do not know what that something is. I have moved 56 times. This means I've lived in 56 different houses in my life. It is not a matter of just packing my clothing and leaving; it means packing up the entire household and moving. It's a large undertaking.

When get to a new place, I love it for a little while. I'll think, *Oh this is so nice! This is so lovely!* Then I start to get uncomfortable. It was never anything I could put my finger on. It was just this indefinable sense of "dis-ease." It's like the field on the other side of the road is always greener. It took many years of this type of behavior before I recognized that I was actually looking for a place where I felt safe and accepted, and also valued and respected.

It took me a long time to figure out that feeling safe is not going to come from external circumstances—it can only come from my internal beliefs about myself. I have now been in my current home for two years, and while I probably will move into a house that does not have so many stairs, I will stay in the same community. I believe I have finally found my true home because I am more comfortable with who I am as a person.

People who have been abused also have difficulty trusting anyone. Even with an intimate partner, this nagging feeling can come up, *Can I trust this person?* perhaps even when you are making love. It can come up when they do not arrive at home on time. It can happen when they look at you and your mind imagines they looked at you in a funny way. It can be a constant and undefined feeling of not being safe, that somehow the person you trust is going to betray you because everybody else in your life has.

Difficulty in trusting can damage your connection with God. The need to be hyper-vigilant makes the world seem hostile, which can lead to believing that God does not care—or at least does not care about you. After all, why would He allow such horrible things to happen in the world if He really loved us?

The topic of abuse is far too large to address adequately here. Look for my next book, *Soul Shift for Survivors—From Victim to Wholehearted Living,* for a deeper exploration of the topic. In this new book, you will learn how to take the steps to a wholehearted life.

The difference between surviving and living a wholehearted life is like the difference between night and day—and many of us do not know how to get there. However, if you have high ACEs, it does not mean you're doomed to failure for the rest of your life. Scientists used to think the brain never changed. The great news is that the brain is capable of regeneration, and the brain and body want to heal. There is a great deal of research that shows how individuals can become healthier through mindfulness practices, exercise, good nutrition, adequate sleep, and healthy social interactions, as well as spiritual practices.

CHAPTER SIX

# Shame
*The Darkness Lurking Within*

## Definitions of Shame:

> "Shame is a painful feeling that is a mix of regret, self-hate, and dishonor. A good person would feel shame if they cheated on a test or did something mean to a friend."
>
> —vocabulary.com

> "Shame is the painful feeling arising from the consciousness of something dishonorable, improper, ridiculous, or so forth done by oneself or another."
>
> —dictionary.com

Perhaps the best definition of shame comes from Brené Brown in *Daring Greatly*:

> "Shame is the intensely painful feeling or experience of believing that we are flawed and, therefore, unworthy of love and belonging."

## The Important Distinction between Shame and Guilt

In today's world, we are beginning to have conversations about the forbidden world of emotion. Shame is a big part of almost everybody's life.

In shame cultures, what matters most is what other people think of you—the embarrassment, the ignominy, and the loss of face. In shame cultures, we are actors playing our part on the public stage and subject to the public's derision. If we are caught doing wrong, there is a stain on our character that might or might not be erased by time. The effects of shame cultures can cross centuries. If your great-grandfather stole his neighbor's cow, the entire family can be stained by his crime for generations.

In guilt cultures, it is what your conscience tells you that matters. We are engaged in inner conversations with our better nature. These conversations are sometimes thought of as conversations with *shoulder angels*. There is a clear distinction between the person who does the deed and the deed itself. There is a difference between the sin and the sinner. Guilt cultures focus on atonement and repentance, apology and forgiveness. The act was wrong, but the character can be redeemed. There is no indelible stain, and the sin committed does not spill over onto innocent family members.

## The Modern Shame Culture

Today, you cannot watch television without seeing somebody being shamed. Everything and everyone is up for scrutiny—their mistakes, their appearance, the way they dress—and the comments can be absolutely vicious.

Cyber-bullying is widespread, and the consequences can be devastating when someone uses the Internet, cell phones, or other technology to send texts or images intended to hurt or embarrass another person.

We have all seen people in the public eye, such as actors or actresses or musicians, who are completely shredded by comments on the Internet regarding the way they look, the way they dress, act, or conduct their relationships. We have become so transparent. All you have to do is enter a question into Google and you can pull up some sort of dirt on almost anybody if you look hard enough.

One of the most notorious cyber-bullying and public humiliations took place for Monica Lewinsky. She writes in *Vanity Fair* on May 6, 2014:

> "Yes, we're all connected now. We can tweet a revolution in the streets or chronicle achievements large and small, but we are also caught in a feedback loop of defame and shame, one in which we have become both perps and victims. We may not have become a crueler society, although it sure feels as if we have, but the Internet has seismically shifted the tone of our interactions—the ease, the speed and the distance that our electronic devices afford us can also make us colder, more glib and less concerned about the consequences of our pranks and prejudices. Having lived humiliation in the most intimate possible way, I marvel at how willingly we have all signed on to this new way of being."

How did it become okay to eviscerate people on the Internet? This is not something we would have done if we were standing with someone face to face. There is a kind of anonymity that goes along with sitting in your room and typing on your computer, attacking somebody who is not in the same space as you.

There is a great deal of shaming going on all around us, and we fall victim to it because of what we learned in our families of origin. These shame triggers cause the most difficulty.

Some of us were told, "Shame on you" when we did something wrong as children. The question, "What would the neighbors think?" trains us to believe that other people are judging us constantly. This creates an unhealthy paradigm, which naturally causes us to assume other people are judging us. It becomes part of our psyche and we develop the paranoid impression that everything we do is up for scrutiny. This statement is never said to us when we do something good, but only when we do something the accuser thinks is bad.

Shame is not actually about a person's behavior. It is about caring what other people *think* about that behavior. It is not something we've done, it is more a reflection of who or what we *are*.

## What Shame Does to a Person Emotionally and Physically

Regardless of what triggers a person when shame is experienced, the deterioration of self-esteem can be devastating. Riding hard on the heels of shame are envy, anger, rage, anxiety, sadness, depression, loneliness, and emptiness. Shame combined with these other powerful emotions can become dangerous. When shame is overwhelming, a person might feel they can never regain a sense of acceptance or worthiness from either themselves or others.

Many people who have been shamed turn to alcohol, drugs, or some other self-destructive behavior to mask or numb their pain. Even worse, how often have we read of some child who has taken his (or her) own life because of being shamed or bullied? How many public figures do we know who have committed suicide because of shame? In many cases, unrelenting public ridicule and cyber-bullying made their life so miserable they couldn't think of any other way out. Their desperate cry for help often fell on deaf ears. These people might have made choices that most of us didn't even know about or might not have noticed, but the media wouldn't let go.

I became aware of the drama surrounding a very talented music artist's choice of clothing. She attended the MTV awards wearing a dress that apparently her critics did not feel was acceptable. Even though she had always received praise up to that point, I was astonished at the vehemence and heat of the conversation that went on around her dress. I thought, *It's just a dress, people! Haven't you ever made a mistake? Was it even a mistake?*

Have you ever gone to school and been made fun of and shamed because your zipper was down or, heaven forbid, you had tucked your shirt into your pants incorrectly?

I was walking down the road at Chico State University in California and saw a woman who had inadvertently tucked her skirt into her pantyhose so that her bottom was hanging out. The ridicule she was getting without anybody telling her what was wrong was shocking. Unfortunately, she was on the other side of a creek and I was biking in the other direction, so I was unable to tell her to adjust her clothing. I felt that yelling across the creek to get her attention—thereby drawing the attention of other people who might not have noticed her—was not the best choice. There was already a lot of catcalling and jeers being shouted at her.

As she was walking, the mocking and laughter appeared to affect her almost like physical blows. She actually seemed to wilt, almost as if she were caving inward on herself—and she didn't even know why these people were making fun of her. She walked faster, until she was practically running toward the nearest building, where she flung open the door and vanished inside.

We are instructed by our culture, by Hollywood, and by our inner authorities as to what our bodies *should* look like. We are told what our eyes should look like and what shape they should be. Our teeth must be straight, pearly white, and perfect. As women, we must all have large full bosoms, tiny waists, and shapely hips. If we fall outside of society's expectations, we often feel ashamed, as though we have failed somehow and are not worthy of being loved just the way we are.

Shame manifests itself in our bodies. When I feel shame, my stomach clenches. I feel bile creeping up my esophagus. A lump forms in my throat and it's difficult to breathe or speak. It feels like somebody has taken a large circular object and shoved it through my chest, and I am unable to breathe around it or be comfortable in my body.

Sometimes I feel it in my face; sometimes as heat in my hair, but I know and recognize the feeling. When I feel shamed, I feel like I can't get any words out in my defense. All I want to do is crawl underneath the carpet or some other place where I can't be found, so I don't have to feel such an intense feeling of being unworthy anymore.

If the shame goes long enough without relief, it definitely affects the way I feel about myself. When I have been shamed, I feel too embarrassed to do any of the things I might have wanted to do before. It makes me feel like I no longer have the courage to attempt something new or step outside of my comfort zone. After all, who am I that anyone would listen to what I have to say?

Shame makes me feel like I absolutely must stay within the rigid structure of somebody else's expectations. I check against my wall, and judging by the feeling in my body, I have obviously embarrassed or offended somebody on my authority wall. I become compliant and very well behaved. I do my best to become completely invisible so I will not be shamed again. The sad thing about this is that even though my authorities are no longer around, their power can still strangle me into submission.

Shame can trigger rage. Anger is a defensive and protective emotion that arises so the person who has offended you does not know how badly you have been hurt. Anger shields hurt. Rage shields feeling unsafe and fearful, which also shields hurt. It is an unconscious way of drawing a bubble around yourself so you can't be hurt any further.

Shame is perhaps the most expensive emotion we experience in terms of loss and opportunity cost. Our shamed inner psyche struggles with thoughts such as, *I'm not good enough*, and asks perverse questions like, *Who do I think I am? Who is going to read this? Who is going to trust me? What made me I think I could accomplish my goal? I don't deserve to have a happy life.* All of these emotions and thoughts are triggered when we experience shame. Imagine what might have been lost if Thomas Edison, Rosa Parks, Indira Gandhi, or Oprah Winfrey had given in to this kind of thinking.

One summer, when my youngest was only two, his favorite movie was Disney's *101 Dalmatians*. He watched it at every opportunity. The wife in the movie calls the husband an "idiot" all the time. She means it as an affectionate term.

We were attending Jeffrey Junior's great-great-grandmother's 90th birthday party. During the party, he would run up to somebody, smile at them, and shout at the top of his lungs, "You idiot!" and then run off to the next person and do it all over again.

I thought I was going to die of embarrassment. In his innocence, he intended to say something loving, but what came out of his mouth shocked everyone, especially his very proper great-great grandmother! These words are deeply socially unacceptable. Of course, the more I tried to shush him, the more he said it. It was a game to him, but I felt shamed, convinced all the relatives were thinking I was a terrible parent.

Here are some things to contemplate:

Shame is feeling we are flawed and, therefore, unworthy of loving or being loved.

Shame holds us back from doing the things we dream of doing. It is like carrying around a backpack full of very heavy rocks. We can't see them because they're inside the pack on our back, but we're always aware they are there. We can always add more rocks, but rarely do we put them down. The weight keeps us from taking risks or changing directions. It almost guarantees we'll stay stuck in our same patterns of behavior.

Shame is a dark, secret feeling that can only control us as long as it is kept in the dark. Suppose we were to put the backpack down, open it up, and bring each "shame stone" out into the light. Oddly enough, shame cannot continue when it is exposed to the light. We could examine the shame stones and try to figure out what was going on in our lives when we first picked them up.

How old were we? Who put the shame stones in our backpack? Do we still want to carry them around, or are we ready to shine a bright light on them until they evaporate and leave us altogether?

Shame is a powerful, dark, and almost slimy emotion that often requires outside help to overcome. It is so close to us, so deep down that a trusted guide is needed to help us shine a bright enough light so it can evaporate.

I find my greatest joy in helping others overcome their shame triggers as they make their Soul Shift.

When did you first feel shame? This would be sometime during your childhood. It might have been when you broke a dish or said something you probably should not have said.

Who was with you? How did they express their disapproval?

Where did you feel shame in your body?

Take a moment to write down the answers to these questions so you can begin to recognize and understand how shame affects you.

CHAPTER SEVEN

# Self-Perception
*The Myth in the Mirror*

"Our culture is obsessed with perfection, especially when it comes to the way women look. The parameters of acceptability as far as physical appearance go are so limiting that only a handful of women actually fall into this category and the rest of us are left to either squeeze ourselves into molds that don't fit, hating ourselves all the while, or we just give up entirely."

—*Yancy Lael*

## Self-Esteem versus Self-Worth

The words "self-esteem" and "self-worth" are often used interchangeably. The difficulty is that these words do not mean the same thing.

Self-esteem is how we feel about ourselves. How others treat us influences how we feel about ourselves, and these two things are in a constant state of flux. If you are other-centered, the opinions of other people will definitely influence the way you feel about yourself. The programming you received as a child contributes to this internal dialog. When other people respond to you in a favorable or unfavorable way, your internal dialog is triggered. You allow it to affect you either in a positive or a negative way. It's your choice.

Self-worth, on the other hand, is the value of our souls, which is our spirit and our body combined. The soul is priceless. Our self-worth, our value, never changes. Our self-worth is our value as a person. It is immeasurable. We are divine creations. We are children of God and, as such, our worth is inestimable.

It is not possible to put a value on the worth of our souls, because they have already been purchased by the blood of the only perfect individual who ever lived on the earth, our Savior, Jesus Christ, the Son of the living God.

Our self-esteem is constantly changing. Self-worth is not. Once we really understand on a deep level how precious we are, just because we *are*, nobody can disturb our equanimity.

Most people are still living at the self-esteem level. In order to achieve complete and full self-esteem, we have to accept full responsibility for our lives, for both our internal and external experiences.

It's easy to fall into the trap of blaming other people for how we feel or for what happens to us because the alternative is to accept responsibility for our actions and responses. We become distracted by looking for solutions to our problems outside of ourselves, or we refuse to look for a solution because we mistakenly believe we cannot help the way we are. Perhaps we tell ourselves, *This is just the way I am.*

Sometimes, a person with good self-esteem is accused of being conceited or selfish and looked down on. Once again, our self-worth is our value. Self-esteem is a feeling, and self-worth is a value. Do you see the difference? Our culture is rife with wonderful people who struggle with self-esteem and self-worth issues.

In our techno world, we are constantly bombarded with media perceptions of what beautiful is, what success means, and what popular signifies. The majority of us cannot meet the mark. Magazines portray images of beautifully airbrushed, flawlessly Photoshopped people, and they become the standard to which we aspire. I don't know about you, but the image I see in my mirror every morning does not look flawless.

For some reason, I have not been able to find a mirror that will Photoshop my image for me so I don't see all the sags, bags, bumps, wrinkles, stretch marks, and scars that are a testament to the life I have lived. Although I would rather not have these visible reminders, I do not regret the experiences in which I gathered them.

My four pregnancies left behind a body covered with silvery, thin-skinned tracks, but I would not trade any of my precious children for even a moment of my pre-pregnancy body—not even if it meant I could wear that really cute swimsuit I keep drooling over. Years of weight fluctuation have left me less than toned, and accidents have left their reminders behind, as well.

I recently acquired a set of six little scars on my abdomen from having cancer removed from my body, forever documenting in my flesh another experience I have lived through. My hair has lots of silvery highlights, my skin is not smooth, and I have grown a strange thing on my lip. Does this mean I am no longer a person of value or worth? Sometimes it feels like it, and *this* is the problem.

It is not how the world perceives me—it is how *I* perceive myself that needs attention.

The other day, I was walking through the grocery store with my husband. He was pushing the cart and I was holding his arm as we strolled through the aisles. There were two men who gave me appreciative looks and comments as we passed them. It's flattering to know I am still attractive, but is that what self-esteem is all about? Is it just about attracting the opposite sex? Certainly not for me! I am happily married, and I cuddled a bit closer to my husband so the two wolves in the market would get the point.

Is it about looking better than the next female so I will get chosen by the male, a sort of peacock in reverse kind of thing? Not for me. I am no longer in the child-bearing mode, so all these survival instinct and reproductive maneuvers are unnecessary, yet I still struggle to feel good enough if I do not look my very best when I go out into the business world.

The illusion is in believing that hitting a certain number on the scale or wearing a certain kind of clothing determines my worth—as if my intelligence or value towards getting the job done would be enhanced if only I had nicer clothes, more jewelry, or drove a sports car. Would my ability to serve others be much improved if I lost weight and got a tummy tuck or a facelift?

Weight issues affect all of us at some point. Either we think we are too fat and struggle with issues regarding weight loss, or we think we are too thin and struggle to gain weight. It is just as devastating being ridiculed for being underweight as it is for being overweight. The reason most of us do not think so is we are not wandering around in the other person's shoes.

Most of our perceptions about our bodies come from somewhere else. Think about it: How many two-year-olds do you see looking at their backsides in the mirror and asking, "Does this diaper make me look fat?" Yet by the time children are five, they are already making judgments about their bodies and beginning to be concerned about their weight.

When we have no solid sense of ourselves and no confidence in our self-perception, other people's opinions become very important to us. Somewhere in our growing-up years what other people said about us took a higher priority than what our feelings and eyesight told us about ourselves.

Carla, a beautiful nine-year-old I know, became anorexic because she got such positive feedback from being "as light as a feather." She had always been tiny, and when she began to grow, as a healthy young lady should, she stopped eating because she was gaining weight.

I remember a classmate making fun of my legs when I was in sixth grade. This was followed by ribbing about the speed (or lack thereof) that I was developing in comparison to the other girls in my class. Later, boyfriends regularly made negative comments about how they wished some part of my body was shaped differently. The most toxic man I ever dated even criticized the way my toenails grew!

Years before Photoshop, I was a model. Modeling is not an easy career. The competition can be vicious. I was often criticized for the way I looked: "If you lost five pounds, you would really be something!" What did they mean by "something?" Did this mean those five pounds made me nothing?

"Maybe if you changed your hairstyle" was the next suggestion. My hair was either too long or too short, depending on what they wanted at the photo shoot. Occasionally, they would complain about the color.

Sometimes, I was told, "You might have a better chance at getting this job if you had your teeth straightened." I have naturally straight teeth, with only one a tiny bit out of alignment.

This went on for quite some time. It seemed like nothing about me was good enough. A scar here, a blemish there, the shape of my feet, my ankles, a dimple on my thigh, the way I filled out a bra. My neck was too long or too perfect, depending on the day or the whims of the person speaking. I looked too young, too old, too something . . . or not enough something.

Enter now the "Age of Photoshop," when we are constantly bombarded by the world's perception of what is beautiful. A leading magazine photographer said he Photoshops 99.9% of the models he photographs because the magazines require it. It seems the nastier and more critical a "beauty expert" is, the more popular they are.

Last year, in the area where my daughter lives, breast enhancement was the gift of choice for young women graduating from high school. What do you think a gift like this says to a young woman? You are not good enough as you are. You need to be "enhanced" in order to get the right job or the right guy. You cannot be your best without a little help.

When you compare yourself to other women, remember you're not seeing the whole picture. Very often the person you are comparing yourself to has been engineered. Undergarments lift, shape, squeeze, and tuck like never before. Plastic surgery is on the rise for every single part of the body, and women spend millions of dollars and hours at the gym trying to sculpt themselves into a different shape. When the mirror doesn't present the image they want to see, they use Photoshop and post the altered versions of themselves online. Why? They want to look good in someone else's eyes.

The opinion of someone else is so important to us that we will go to almost any length to change what God gave us because we believe, deep down, that His work is imperfect. We believe that somehow in the eyes of the world we are not good enough. We believe the lies that tell us we would feel better about ourselves if we turned more heads while walking down the street, and that everyone else is more beautiful than we are.

The child-bearing years are brutal. Not only do we fret about how much weight we gain with each pregnancy, we get stretch marks, strange blotches on our skin, our hips spread, and everything sags. Instead of looking at ourselves in the full-length mirror with love and pride at what we have accomplished, recognizing how beautiful we are, we grieve for the unscarred bodies we will never be able to reclaim.

We weep because we believe we have become ugly.

This is compounded beyond measure if your husband, the guy who promised to love and cherish you for the rest of forever, becomes addicted to pornography. Any self-esteem you might have managed to salvage evaporates like mist in a heat wave.

All of a sudden, your belief that you are ugly and not good enough is proven to be true because, obviously, if you were beautiful and good enough your husband would not be looking at other women.

Let me interject that addiction to pornography is not about you, really—it is about him. He has some demons he has not dealt with, and it probably is not even about sex. But this is not the way it *feels* when you discover he has been unfaithful to you—and do not mistake this: he *has* been unfaithful.

Multiple virtual mistresses are just as emotionally difficult to deal with as flesh and blood women.

Suppose you discover your husband has been unfaithful to your marriage covenants. How does it make you feel—ugly, fat, and undesirable?

You chase yourself around in your head with thoughts of, *Maybe if I lost some weight, or dressed sexier, or wore my hair differently, or tried to be sweeter* (although you are already the sweetest woman on the planet) *then he would really love me, find me desirable, and stop looking at all those other women.*

Every time he says, "I love you," you do not believe him. Every time he says, "You are beautiful," you do not believe him.

You survive the crisis of infidelity and discover one day that gravity has become your worst enemy. You have wrinkles, and you can relate far too well to the children's book *The Saggy Baggy Elephant*.

Along life's journey, you have picked up physical scars you believe mar your beauty, and the unseen emotional scars are beyond description.

As I was complaining about my body one day in my late 20s, my mother told me the day would come when I would give anything in the world to have that body back. Of course, I thought she was nuts and, of course, she was absolutely right.

The pressure on women to look perfect is unrelenting, but there is also pressure on men, and because of our culture this is escalating. The phrase "men should be tall, dark, and handsome" is the standard. They should be muscular, strong, have six-pack abs, and definitely not have man boobs. Plastic surgery for men is a thriving business, as they struggle to fit into a mold that is just as constricting, painful, and unrealistic as the one constructed for women.

If men are dreaming of a pin-up model, women are dreaming of a male stripper or the god Adonis. Most of us don't fall into either category.

Eventually, we arrive at an age when things stop working in our bodies—our knees hurt, our hips will not work the way they used to, the wrinkles deepen, our eyesight gives us trouble, and our hair leaps from our heads in handfuls like rats abandoning a sinking ship. As my dad used to say, "Aging ain't for sissies."

We tend to judge people based on their value. We assign a value to someone we see or meet—a homeless person we pass on the street has less value for us than a coworker, so we ignore or dismiss them.

Our family members have different values for us. Perhaps a wayward sibling has less value than a beloved, obedient child. Perhaps we admire our sister's husband more than we do our own. Does a struggling child have as much place in our hearts as the one who is easier to live with?

The trick is to understand that we are all of equal value to our Heavenly Father. He sees each of us as His beloved child. To Him, the homeless person on the street has no less value than the child who keeps all the commandments and lives a righteous life. The person who chooses to walk in the path of our Savior receives more blessings, but this does not mean he (or she) is more important or more valued.

It is a natural consequence to an irrevocable law that the righteous receive the greater blessings, while those who choose evil do not. It is not capriciousness on the part of God.

What would happen if we looked at every single person we came across in our daily activities as having equal value? What miracles could come to pass if we really learned to love as our Savior loved?

My husband has a ladder that he gets in a fight with nearly every time he uses it. One day, he was painting a ceiling using the ladder. I didn't say anything because I really do try not to boss him around; however, when he fell off the ladder, I was not surprised. I ran into the room and saw paint all over my brand new carpet.

Can you imagine how the rest of the day might have gone if I had placed more value on the carpet than on my husband's well being?

## The Difference between What We See and What Others See

A few months ago, I noticed the gardenia bush outside the grocery store was in bloom. I picked up a gardenia blossom the wind had blown off and held it to my nose. It smelled absolutely amazing. I tucked it into my purse and went inside.

Near the door, there were packages of absolutely perfect roses. They had beautiful petals and few visible flaws, unless you looked really closely, but not one rose in the store had any fragrance.

Compare this to the gardenia from outside of the store. A gardenia has funny, misshapen petals, and yet the fragrance is strong and beautiful. Once the flower is dry, the gardenia continues to have that beautiful scent, and it can last for a very long time. I have carried a dried gardenia around with me for the last seven years and I can still smell the fragrance.

On the other hand, I also have some dried roses I've kept as a memento of my wedding and they smell like dust.

When asked to think of a beautiful flower, most people immediately think of a rose, but I would choose the gardenia every time, regardless of its flaws and how funny it looks.

That is what people are like. Are you a rose or a gardenia? Do you have strength and fragrance and beauty to offer, or are you almost plastic-like and smell like dust?

## The Mirror Exercise

One morning, when I was a teenager, I was walking past my mother's mirror. I glanced at it and was shocked to see what appeared to be somebody else staring back at me. I stopped in amazement and looked in the mirror more closely. It was as though the image in the mirror was trying to get my attention.

I stopped and said, "What?" It seemed as though I could hear the image in the mirror say back to me, "It is about time you noticed me."

I felt terribly foolish, but I began to have a conversation with the girl in the mirror. I complemented her on the maturity with which she had handled a problem with her older brother that morning. Getting into the spirit of this strange experience, I sat on the edge of the bed and discussed a wide variety of topics: school, my boyfriend, and what I wanted to be when I grew up. The image in the mirror listened attentively. When I was done, I shyly said, "I love you" to the girl in the mirror. It felt amazing. For the first time in my life I felt like I had truly been listened to and heard by someone who wanted only good things for me. I repeated this experience twice. I can't help but wonder how different my life would have been if I had continued having this conversation on a regular basis.

Imagine my surprise when I learned that the mirror exercise is a tool for building self-esteem. Everyone needs to hear kind, loving, and encouraging things about themselves, so why not say these things while looking in a mirror? It will help you feel better about yourself, accept your limitations, and become your own cheerleader.

Every night before you go to bed, look in the mirror. Look deeply into the eyes of the image you see. For many of you, even this will be uncomfortable. When you've made eye contact, have a conversation with yourself. You might need to explain what you're trying to do because, trust me, it feels really strange to be doing this if you've never done it before.

You also might warn anyone else who lives in your house so they don't wonder why you are talking to yourself.

Acknowledge yourself for all the good things you have done during the day. Perhaps you did not lose your temper in a tense situation. Perhaps you showed kindness to someone who was troubled. Perhaps you did not eat that extra cookie. Whatever positive actions you want to acknowledge, tell the image in the mirror how proud you are of your success. Talk about your dreams and how excited you are to attain them. The only rule is that you must say only positive things about the person into whose eyes you are staring.

This conversation can be short or long, but when you are finished the last thing to say as you look deeply into your own eyes in the mirror is, "I love you."

This exercise is going to be very uncomfortable for many of you, but if you do it consistently for 40 days, your life will change. If you miss a day, you begin counting again from the beginning. Keep it up until you accomplish having this loving conversation for the full 40 days. If you compliment yourself about the positive things you have done and talk to yourself about your dreams and how your life will look when you accomplish them, your life *will* change.

When you tell yourself you love you, eventually you really will begin to love yourself. Even if you are living in an atmosphere where nobody ever says anything nice to you, as your own champion and cheerleader you are going to begin feeling a shift in your soul.

CHAPTER EIGHT

# Relationships
*How to Get Off the Merry-Go-Round*

**Definition of Relationship:** "The way in which two or more people or things are connected with or involve each other."

—macmilliandictionary.com

## Managing the Crowds

When you are having a conversation with someone, you probably think you are only talking with one person. In reality, you are also speaking with their parents, their grandparents, siblings, and everyone who has written on their wall. They are also speaking to you and those who have written on *your* wall. It can get quite crowded and difficult to figure out exactly who you are talking with at any given moment.

If you have been in a long-term relationship, you might have noticed this phenomenon. Occasionally, your partner might respond to a stressful situation in exactly the same way as their mother or father would respond. This might be okay with you if it aligns with what's on your wall, or it might cause problems. I have been known to stop a conversation with my husband and say, "Wait, who am I talking to here?" When I ask this question, he is able to step back, take a deep breath, and identify which of his authorities took over the conversation at that moment. I can get away with saying this because he is also aware of the phenomenon.

Gently making your partner aware that they are exhibiting the behaviors of their parent(s) can sometimes help if you are both aware of this possibility. However, it would probably be best if you taught them this concept when you are *not* having a disagreement.

People always do the best they can with the limited awareness, knowledge, and skill they have at the moment to meet their basic needs. When they have more awareness, knowledge, and skills, they will be able to meet their basic needs in a more elegant way.

What do you do when you live with someone who does not believe you can change your beliefs or behaviors, or who actively puts up a fight when you attempt to do so? What happens when you "rock the boat" or change the status quo?

When I was talking with my psychologist all those years ago, she warned me that as I tried to make changes, my life with my significant other would most likely become more difficult. After all, he had entered into a relationship with me as the person I was at the time, and he liked me that way.

The harder I tried to change, the harder he tried to make me remain the same. He was not a bad person. This is just the way people interact with each other. He was comfortable with me the way I was, and my efforts to change were threatening.

On one occasion, during a rather noisy argument, he said he hated my psychologist because she had made me different. I laughed. *She* had not *made* me different. She had only shown me it was okay to acknowledge my pain, and that it was possible to change my unhappy circumstances.

The changes were coming from inside me. I looked at who I was and who I wanted to be, and I liked the changes I was making. I was more confident, more independent, and I took better care of myself. However, the person I was becoming was *not* the person my significant other wanted me to be, and our relationship became conflicted.

Eventually, I had to make a choice—I could either revert back to my former self in order to maintain the relationship, or be true to myself and protect the happiness I had found within. I chose happiness and terminated that relationship.

I am not suggesting that you automatically jettison your relationships. It is difficult to maintain a relationship with another person for any length of time. Once you get past the "honeymoon phase," the real work starts. However, in order to attain your Soul Shift, it is important to have supportive people around you.

Invite the important people in your life to join with you in the adventure of discovering who you really are and living the kind of life you really want to live. Along the way, they might discover who *they* really are and live the life *they* want to live. It can be an enriching experience for everyone involved.

I adore my husband. We have been married for over 21 years. During this time, we have faced horrendous challenges. There were things I would never have put up with had they happened with anyone else, yet I have never considered jettisoning my relationship with him because he is my best friend.

We work together. Sometimes he changes, sometimes I change, sometimes we work together to change our circumstances, but each of us is a work in progress and we lovingly support each other. He knows I am continually evolving, and he is supportive in my efforts to clear out my toxic emotional baggage.

He is not always comfortable with the changes that happen within me, however, because it often triggers *his* issues and then *he* has to get back to work.

In our families, we all have jobs or roles that are either given to us, or we take them on voluntarily in order to find some kind of peace and acceptance. Whenever a new person comes into the family, there is a kind of mental shuffling that goes on as everyone seeks to find his (or her) place in the new structure.

Observant parents who have brought home a new baby see the shifting take place in the eyes of their older children as they struggle to adjust to their amended place in the family.

For example, my second daughter was barely 19 months old when I brought my newborn son home. The pain she experienced was obvious, as she struggled to adjust in her own mind to this little interloper, whom she adored, but who demanded so much of her mommy's attention.

Even though I tried to prepare her beforehand for the new arrival and was careful to give her as much attention as I possibly could after her brother's birth, I could clearly see the struggle going on inside of her by looking at her drawn features, the dark circles under her eyes, and the way she carried herself.

It only lasted a few days and then she bounced back, but it was clear there had been a shift in her mind as to where she belonged in the family.

I witnessed a similar shift years later as my three teenaged children adjusted to the birth of their baby brother. The one who previously had the favored place of baby of the family had some adjusting to do, as did we all. It is tough to be dethroned at the age of 13!

It is also tough on your self-esteem to have people comment on what a cute couple you and your sister are and what an adorable baby you have. I agree. Our 15-year-old daughter and 13-year-old son were a cute couple of kids, and our brand new baby was adorable. However, more than once, if we were shopping and they wandered off to a different part of the store with our baby in their arms, they would return, red-faced and indignant because someone had assumed they were teenaged parents.

On the first Sunday at church in a new town, our daughter showed remarkable skill in recognizing how important first impressions are in making new relationships. She unbuckled the baby from his car seat and handed him to me. "I am *not* going to carry him inside," she stated. "I am *not* going to start off here with people thinking he's mine!" She gave us a beautiful smile, and then turned and led the way into the building.

What was your job or place in your family of origin? Were you the responsible one? Were you the peacekeeper, the holder of the family secrets, the scapegoat, or everyone else's parent, including the adults? Were you daddy's sweetheart or mommy's darling? Were you invisible? Were you the target? Were you outcast because of your parentage?

Did your role change because of circumstances? For example, did your position in the family change because your parent remarried and there were new children to contend with—either step-siblings or half-siblings? Did things change because your stepparent did not like you? Did your parent dislike you because you reminded him (or her) of the despised former partner?

What if your parents went through a divorce and emotionally checked out or fell apart, and suddenly *you* were the responsible one who kept everything together?

All of these things can seriously mess with your self-concept, and if you do not replace the negative feedback you received with loving, supportive feedback that you give yourself, you will continue to struggle with finding peace in your daily life.

## Family—Biological versus Selected

We are trained to believe that blood is thicker than water. We are taught that a family member must always defend and protect the family in all circumstances, no matter what. It is either stated or implied that anything we say against our family of origin is a deep betrayal and shameful breach of trust—and heaven help us if we expose the family secrets. Somehow, we have betrayed the family honor if we've told the family's deepest, darkest secrets.

We are trained to believe that our families are the most important people in the world and we must defend them at all cost. How many of us are torn between defending our family of origin and the family we have created? How many in-law relationships are painful and toxic?

A family does not have to be made up of people you are related to biologically. The most important man in my life as a child was my grandfather, Clayton. He was not related to me. He was my grandmother's third husband, but I knew he loved me unconditionally. He was the only emotionally healthy male I had ever interacted with, and he probably saved my life from being worse than it was.

The man I claim as my father was my mother's last husband. I first met him when I was 12. I was already an adult and no longer lived at home when mom finally married Larry. He was always there for me, supportive and kind.

After I graduated high school, I lived for a time with a family who took me in as if I were one of their own. While I lived with them, I got to see how a healthy father and mother interacted with each other and with their children. I learned that it was possible to be firm, yet loving at the same time. Their example has always been my litmus test for my own parenting, and I will be eternally grateful to them for the years I knew and loved them.

You can choose who you want to call "family." Who are the people who love, nurture, protect, and support you? It does not matter if they are not related to you by blood. They are related to you by heartstrings, which are stronger than blood can ever be. Is your family of choice the family you were born into, or are they people you have chosen because of the heart connection you share?

## Negative and Positive People

Changes bring challenges. When you enter a relationship, you bring the person you are at that very moment into the relationship. Your partner likes you this way because it is what attracted them to you in the first place.

When you try to make changes, the challenges are going to come. Is your partner or family member going to be supportive of you, or are they going to do everything they can to sabotage your progress so you will return to "normal?" Are they going to try to force you back into the kind of relationship you had with them before?

Make a list of all of the people you interact with on a regular basis and put a plus sign next to their names if they are a positive influence in your life. If they are a negative influence, put a minus sign next to their names. If they are kind of both, put a plus-or-minus next to them.

Now look at your list again. How often do you hang out with the positive people, those who support and love you, accept and encourage you?

Look at the people with a minus sign by their names. How often do you hang out with them? How much time do you spend with people who put you down, control you, are not encouraging, and are not loving in their interactions with you? It can be disturbing to discover that your siblings, parents, or possibly even your own children drag you down because of their negativity.

It is very important to spend as little time as possible with the people who are negative. Just doing the exercise and mindfully thinking about these people and putting a plus or minus by their names can be an eye-opening exercise.

If you choose to be with the people who are loving and supportive, you will have the opportunity to blossom and grow.

If you choose to be with the people who are negative, you will need to fight every step of the way to grow and change your circumstances. Who would you rather be with? Would you rather be stuck in the mud, or would you rather be soaring to new heights?

## Permission to Choose Better

Jettisoning people from our relationships can conflict with the writing on our walls that tell us families are sacred and they are to be protected. If your relationship with your mother is difficult, then restricting the amount of time you spend interacting with her is probably a good idea.

If you need someone's permission to jettison the negative people in your life, then have this conversation with yourself in the mirror. You are the best person to give yourself permission to do anything.

If I were doing it for myself, I would look in the mirror and say, "Hi, Michelle! How is your day going today?" I would still follow the usual mirror exercise protocol and tell myself how much I had accomplished during the day and how proud I am for the things I had done that were good.

Then I would say, "I would like to discuss your relationship with so-and-so. It is a very negative relationship and it causes you tremendous pain. I know that if you try to limit your relationship with this person, there will probably be some painful repercussions, but I also know you are worthy of being loved. You are worthy of being cherished; you are worthy of being encouraged; and you are worthy of having the opportunity to grow—and I love you."

Give yourself verbal permission to limit any particular relationship or, if necessary, jettison it.

## Guilt versus Regret

Guilt and regret are often confused. Guilt is a powerful emotion; regret is milder.

Guilt is the result of having a belief about how you should or should not behave, and taking action—or not taking action—violates your belief. This would be something you did that you felt you shouldn't have done because it was morally or legally wrong. To get rid of guilt, you must change either your belief or your actions. Remember, you cannot change your past actions; you can only choose how you will behave in your present and your future. You can, however, change what you *believe* about your past actions.

Regret is feeling an overwhelming sadness about your behavior or actions, but it is the correct term for something that happened that you have no control over.

Ingrid chose not to continue a relationship with her biological father because of the abuse she suffered at his hands. When she had children, she didn't want to take the chance that he would abuse them in the same manner. She had no control over her father's behavior. She told me she felt guilty, but she could not see any other way to protect herself and her children. When I explained the difference between guilt and regret, she was able to understand she had not done anything morally or legally wrong, but that she regretted her children were missing out on having a grandfather.

Both of these emotions relate to events that are in the past. Both of them can throttle and control you. I invite you to take 100% Responsibility for your life from this moment on.

If you have done something in the past that you should not have done, and it was morally or legally wrong, then do what you need to do to make restitution and let it go. Let God take it away from you. Promise you will be a better, wiser person and you will not continue these actions.

If you have a negative relationship with a family member and he (or she) is still around, you might feel guilty about it if the breach really is your fault. Perhaps you regret all the years that have gone by. You can make the choice to start today to make a new kind of relationship.

If it is a toxic relationship and you know it would be best not to continue or resume it, you can have a "conversation with a chair." This healing exercise also works really well if you had a toxic relationship with a deceased family member or a former lover. It is best to do this exercise when no one else is around.

Place a sturdy chair in the center of the room. If you have a picture of the person you have a toxic relationship with, put the picture on the seat of the chair. If you don't have a picture, just use your imagination and visualize the person sitting on the chair.

Begin by telling the person you imagine in the chair about all of the things you are thinking and feeling about your relationship with him (or her). You might tell the person how he (or she) hurt you: *You were never there for me. You hurt me. You hit me. You lied to me. You betrayed me*—whatever emotion you are feeling, let it out. If this is scary or uncomfortable, remind yourself that you are perfectly safe. In real time and space, there isn't anyone in the chair.

Use your angry voice, the one you would normally use when you are really angry. Allow the imaginary person sitting in the chair know how you feel about him (or her) and how you feel about what has been done to you. There is no need to hold back if you feel like swearing. Let it all go. If you feel the need to be physical, get a towel and hit the seat of the chair as hard as you can with the towel.

Once you have exhausted your powerful emotions and you really have nothing left to say, you can move on. Tell the person in the chair how you would rather they had behaved. *I would rather you had loved me. All I wanted you to do was love me. All I wanted you to do was protect me. You are my (parent). You should have protected me.*

After you have gotten these feelings out, the feeling of forgiveness will come. You could say, "I forgive you for not being there for me. Apparently you were not able to love or care for me."

Going though this emotional process without having an actual confrontation with someone in person allows you to be in a safe place, yet say all the things you wanted to say but couldn't. The key is to get rid of the emotions that are trapped and stuck inside of you. The person you imagined in the chair has their own baggage to deal with and you are not responsible for their behavior.

Amy was unable to get any work done in her home office. When visiting there, I noticed there was a picture of her mother hanging on the wall that had not been there before. I asked her what kind of a relationship she had with her mother.

Amy told me her mom had died a few years ago, but they had never had a good relationship. Her mother had been critical and unkind, especially about Amy's weight. It was the first and last topic her mother asked her about in every conversation.

I told Amy about the chair exercise. She was excited to try it and said she would do it as soon as our meeting was over. The next time I talked to Amy, she told me she was thrilled with the results of the exercise. Her productivity had returned to normal. After the chair exercise, she felt lighter and happier. Not only that, she had moved her mother's picture to a little-used room where she can access it when another issue from her past with her mother comes up, but it is not energetically looming over her while she is trying to get her work done.

Come to peace with yourself about your past relationships and you will not have to worry about them anymore. It's a simple exercise, but powerful in its results. Doing this exercise can help you get over the limiting beliefs that were imprinted on your wall by the person with whom you had a toxic relationship.

When you were raised in your home, you became accustomed to the way you were treated. You might not have liked it, but it *was* normal. Your life might have seemed completely abnormal to your friends, depending on what kind of home they were raised in. When you left home, you unconsciously sought out the people and places that made you feel *normal* again.

A vacuum is formed whenever we make changes in our lives. If we do not replace old habits and beliefs with new ones, we will revert right back into the same kind of situation we just left as soon as we can, because anything else feels uncomfortable.

When you begin to eliminate the toxic emotions stuck in your body, you will be better able to choose what kinds of relationships you want to have. You will no longer be carrying around all that old programming. You won't be automatically drawn to people who will treat you badly. You will begin to live a life by conscious choice, rather than by whichever direction the wind blows—and you will be much happier.

CHAPTER NINE

# Addictions

> **Definition of Addiction:** "Addiction is a primary chronic disease of brain reward, motivation, memory and related circuitry. Dysfunction in these circuits leads to characteristic biological, psychological, social and spiritual manifestations. This is reflected in an individual pathologically pursuing reward and/or relief by substance use and other behaviors."
>
> —*American Society of Addiction Medicine*, www.asam.org

## The Brain's Reward Center and Addictions

The reward center of the brain exists for good reason. It is a survival mechanism. If there was not some *this makes me feel good* system, we would have all starved to death as infants, because we would not have cared whether we ate or not. The reward center also ensures that humans will continue to reproduce.

Although you might have heard the term "addictive personality," it is not actually a psychiatric diagnosis. Personalities are very complex. There is not any one person about whom you can nod your head knowingly and say, "Oh yes, that person has an addictive personality." However, there are several factors that can combine to make a person more likely to be addicted.

Trauma in the life of a young person is almost a guarantee they will struggle with some form of addiction. They will seek anything that enables them to feel better, because they did not get the pleasure stimulation they needed to form healthy attachments to people and things. Trauma at any age sets a person up for addiction. We all seek a pathway out of pain.

Even if we do not struggle with addiction to a great degree, at one time or another we will all be tempted by some sort of substance or behavior that wants to suck us into addiction.

## Different Types of Addictions — Not Always What You Expect

The usual things that come to mind when we think of addiction are alcohol, sex, drugs, tobacco, pornography, and food, but there are other things we sometimes do not recognize as addictive.

Chocolate is considered a food, and we think of it as fairly harmless. However, there are chemical compounds in chocolate that stimulate the reward center of the brain, and eating it in excess can be addicting.

Sugar. Just like chocolate, we think of it as fairly harmless, but the world's obesity and diabetes epidemics are related to the amount of sugar we ingest.

Computers. Does this sound ridiculous? Can you really be addicted to your computer? When you open your computer and turn it on, do you get sucked into a black hole of information and places to hide? Do you mentally turn off the outside world?

Cell phones. How many people are addicted to their cell phones? Have you ever wondered what you did with yourself before you had a cell phone? If you check it every few minutes, don't interact with the people around you, and feel a sense of panic when you can't find your phone, you are probably addicted to it.

People can even be addicted to enemas—or anything else that numbs the pain of their lives. Addictions enable a person to "hide" so they don't have to interact with others. Addictions also provide an adrenaline rush of excitement and thrills, or guilty pleasure.

Many years ago, we bought a house that was 98 years old. It was in such bad shape that our neighbor suggested we have a housewarming and use real matches! Rather than using matches, we used hammers and crowbars and tore the house down to the studs, rebuilt the foundation, and then built the house basically from scratch. We provided all the labor, assisted occasionally by friends and members of our church.

It was an extremely stressful time in our lives. The day we ripped off the back of the house, my husband lost his job. We had just taken on a larger mortgage and half of our house was literally gone, including the only bathroom and the kitchen. There were six of us in our family. We were using a port-a-potty and a travel trailer that a kind friend had lent us. We ate our meals on the grass outside and three of us slept in the travel trailer—the other three slept in tents.

We were desperately trying to get the half of the house that was left standing livable before winter. We started the project at the end of July, but by the first frost of October, our oldest son was still living in a tent out by the barn.

Needless to say, we were all under a great deal of stress. While we were rebuilding the house, I kept a secret stash of chocolate candy bars. I kept it hidden away for the times I felt most stressed, or when I felt I deserved a reward for working so hard during the day.

One day, when I was feeling particularly stressed at about 3:00 in the afternoon, I went to my usual hiding places for some chocolate. It was all gone. I nearly tore the house apart looking for even a little piece of chocolate. I looked in every one of my hiding places two or three times, but there wasn't even a crumb.

I looked down at my hands and realized that I was visibly shaking. I was astonished and I muttered in disbelief, *Michelle, you have a serious problem. You are actually addicted to chocolate.*

It took me a while to get over this addiction. For several months I had withdrawal, and at 3:00 every afternoon I would get the shakes. I did a rigorous cleanse to get all of the sugar out of my system, and I did not buy any more chocolate. I used prayer and willpower, and I was able to overcome my addiction. I am grateful I had not chosen to use a stronger substance.

## Recognize Your Triggers

The things that trigger my addictive behaviors are anger, anxiety, and boredom. Sometimes it's a feeling that I need to hide because the world is just too overwhelming. I might stare at the computer all day. I can get absolutely lost in Facebook or just poking around on the Internet for hours and hours, rationalizing that I am *learning something*. Meanwhile, I am totally disconnected from my body.

How often do you get out of your body so you do not have to feel uncomfortable feelings? What do you use to numb your anxieties?

## Taking the Edge Off—Addictive Compulsion

The next time you find yourself reaching for your fix, whatever your substance happens to be, stop a moment and ask yourself, "What am I feeling right now?" Sometimes the compulsion to seek an addictive substance is so strong that you will not be able to overcome it. Begin to recognize what triggers your addictive behaviors and work on prevention.

I have found that tapping is very useful to take the edge off my anxiety and dial down the intensity. I rapidly tap on my collarbone with two fingers when I'm about to give in to addiction.

I redirect myself while tapping to make a different choice for something that is a little healthier, such as an apple or maybe just a drink of water.

I also stop, walk away, and redirect my attention to something else. Before you reach for your addiction, you can choose to stop, turn around, and walk away. Just doing this requires extreme willpower, but it works for most substances unless you are deeply addicted.

Food addictions are one of the most difficult addictions to overcome. It's not like you can go cold turkey and just not eat anymore. You have to eat in order to stay alive. Eating disorders like anorexia and bulimia are addictive/compulsive behaviors rooted in a poor sense of self-esteem. They might also have roots in trauma.

If you have an addiction, it is extremely important to get help, because most likely by the time you realize you have a problem the compulsion to engage in destructive behavior has become part of your cellular structure. There is no shame in seeking help for an addiction. It doesn't mean you are weak or disgusting, or anything like that. It means you are in pain, and the way you are choosing to deal with the pain is not healthy. If you had a visible wound, you would rush to ask for help. Asking for help for invisible wounds is a sign of strength, not weakness.

We all have an addiction of one kind or another, so you are just like everybody else and it really is okay.

People relapse back into addictive behaviors when their underlying emotional issue has not been dealt with. It is essential to discover what trauma has been embedded in your cells and get rid of it. Think of this as a good housecleaning. Everyone feels better in a clean house. The same applies to a clean mind and body.

CHAPTER TEN

# The Pain Point

> "If you always do what you've always done,
> you'll always get what you've always got."
>
> —*Henry Ford*

## How Much Does It Have to Hurt before You Want to Change Your Life?

Every one of us has a "pain point." When we reach this place inside of ourselves, we say, *This is painful—it's more than I can bear and I need to do something about it.*

We could be talking about physical, emotional, intellectual, or spiritual pain. Everybody's pain point is different, and it is different for us in each of these categories.

Some people might be able to tolerate a lot of physical pain, but once something emotionally traumatic happens they fall apart. Perhaps they are emotionally resilient, but something happens to test their faith and they become shakier than a plate of jelly in the middle of a herd of elephants.

It's obvious that someone is in pain or had a painful experience when their arm is in a cast, or perhaps they are bleeding. A visible bruise or a missing arm or leg is proof of a traumatic injury. It is easy to be sympathetic towards people who go into surgery and come out with stitches. For some reason, a physical injury or illness is an acceptable form of weakness to many of us. However, when someone is suffering spiritual or emotional pain, we usually cannot see outward evidence of it. This does not diminish the reality of their experience. They truly are in pain, but in most cultures it is not acceptable to talk about the invisible pains.

The pain point is when the pain is so great we decide we must do something to make it go away, or at least make it more tolerable. At this "point," we are compelled by pain to either change our lives or to engage in behaviors that mask it.

Have you ever listened to someone go on and on about something they do not like about their life? They constantly complain, but they don't do anything about it. This is usually because they either have not reached their pain point, or they are getting something valuable from having people listen to their complaining.

If you have not reached your pain point, you might not be willing to do the work necessary to find your personal peace and experience the Soul Shift that can come from diligent effort. If your pain brings you some emotional gain, you might not want to get rid of it.

A psychologist walked around the room while teaching stress management to an audience. She raised a glass of water, and everybody expected the question they would hear next would be, "Is the glass half empty or half full?" Instead, she asked, "How heavy is this glass of water?"

People looked at it carefully. Their guesses ranged from 8 to 20 ounces. She said, "The absolute weight does not matter. It depends on how long I hold it. If I hold it for a minute, it is not a problem. If I hold it for an hour, I will have an ache in my arm. If I hold it for a day, my arm will feel numb and paralyzed. In each case, the weight of the glass does not change, but the longer I hold it the heavier it becomes."

She continued, "The stresses and worries in life are like this glass of water. Think about them for a while, and nothing happens. Think about them for a bit longer, and they begin to hurt, and if you think about them all day long, you will feel paralyzed, incapable of doing anything. It is important to remember to let go of your stresses. As early in the evening as you can, put your burdens down. Do not carry them through the evening and into the night."

I always cringe when somebody says, "They brought it on themselves" when something catastrophic takes place. We live in this world and we are affected by other people's choices, as well as by the fury of nature.

If you are thinking positive thoughts and working towards a Soul Shift, and you always look for the good in others—most importantly in yourself—and something bad happens to you, it is not your fault. You are only accountable for the choices *you* make, the actions *you* take, and the thoughts *you* think.

My husband used to work in the education system. Every few months, a new kid would show up at school. When the parents met with my husband, they would explain that they were changing schools because their child had been hanging out with the wrong crowd. They were certain the new school would make all the difference, but they were devastated when their child got in with the wrong crowd again and all the former problems reemerged at the new school. He tried to explain to the frustrated parents that the problem was not the school. Their child had brought some emotional baggage with him (or her) to the new school, and until these issues were addressed the child's behavior was not going to improve.

## We Get What We Focus On

So what do you expect? Do you expect the world to be a frightening, horrible place? Do you expect people to be mean and dishonest, take advantage of you or hurt you? If this is what you expect, this is what you are going to get, because these kinds of people will recognize that you are a victim and they will be happy to prey on you.

On the other hand, if you expect people to be good, honest, and friendly, and that everybody in the world is basically good, then your day will be filled with meeting exactly the kinds of people you expect to meet. You might meet the other kinds of people, too, but you will be less likely to notice them.

It is more about your attitude regarding what goes on in your life than about controlling everything. You cannot control what happens to you, no matter how much you would like to.

Strive to think positively about the unpleasant things that happen to you, see them as a chance to grow and stretch, and maintain integrity within yourself to be a good person, and you will be blessed by God and the Universe.

I have a friend who, when something challenging happens, exclaims, "Oh, look! Another opportunity for growth!"

What kinds of thoughts do you have running through your head at any given moment? Let us think about your health. Are you exercising because you want to be fit, healthy, and have energy to enjoy life, or do you exercise because your dad died of a heart attack and you are afraid it might happen to you?

When you have a twinge in your bowel are you afraid you might have cancer? When you have a small lymphatic lump somewhere in your body—which is likely a result of toxins that are not being flushed properly—do you immediately fear the worst?

Imagine you have been diagnosed with something serious and your doctor says you have six months to live? Is your first inclination to believe the doctor? Who went and made your doctor God?

There are countless stories of people who were diagnosed with cancer and given a short period of time to live, but they beat the odds because they refused to believe the cancer was incurable. There are countless other people who died within one or two days of the date the doctor said they would.

## Staying Stuck

Sometimes the benefits of staying stuck are greater than the benefits of recovering from painful experiences. Sometimes, people do not want to get well because illness gives them some kind of emotional benefit that outweighs the benefits of being healthy. People seem to particularly like being told their illnesses are a "rare form" of whatever it is.

Years ago, I knew three people who were diagnosed with a *rare* form of an illness within a couple of weeks of each other. They were three different illnesses, but they were each given the specific term, "a rare form of." It was interesting to watch these people cherish their rare diagnoses.

Please do not mistake what I am saying—they *do* and *did* have terrible, painful, debilitating, life-threatening illnesses. I am not intending to demean their experiences. I am pointing out that sometimes an illness gives a person benefits they would not get in health.

The first person was a woman who had been given a grim prognosis of a rare and painful and degenerative disease. One day, I suggested that she might have a good chance of overcoming her illness and being whole and healthy again if she made a few changes in her lifestyle. She vehemently said, "Oh, no! I will have this disease until the day I die!"

I was puzzled as to why she would choose this path, until I observed her social interactions. A great fuss was being made about her bravery, how patient she is in her affliction, and how much others wish they could have her fortitude in the face of such a difficult trial. She is made comfortable; every whim is fulfilled by the people around her. She positively glows as she drinks in the attention of her peers. Perhaps most important of all, her formerly flirtatious husband has ceased paying attention to other women and is solicitous to her needs.

She is right. She will have that disease until the day she dies. She loves it. It gives her a great deal of benefit, and to be without it would be unthinkable. Perhaps for the first time in her life, she is the center of attention. The loss of that adulation and praise would probably be more painful than the disease itself.

The second person was given a diagnosis of a rare form of PTSD. She, too, was not interested in overcoming her illness but milked it for all she was worth, telling the story of the horror she witnessed to whomever would listen. It really was a very horrific experience. However, because of the benefit she received, she had no interest in overcoming her PTSD and moving on with her life. Rather, she nurtured it because it rewarded her with attention and sympathy.

The third person was diagnosed with a rare form of cancer and was given six months to live. When he first told me of his diagnosis, he also told me the tragic progression of the disease the doctor told him to expect and the timeline for the expected events. I was devastated by his stoic acceptance.

He bravely took up his cross and met each of these milestones on time—the tumors growing bigger, a limb being amputated, and finally the tumors spreading throughout his body. He died exactly six months later.

Why do we never imagine ourselves catching *good* health? We do not come down with a sunny disposition or have a relapse of cheerfulness. We do not anticipate that we are going to suddenly have an abundance of love in our hearts or calm in our colons.

What would happen in your life if you got rid of the continuous emotional pain? How would you feel about yourself if you no longer carried the depression and the overwhelm? How would your family members perceive you if you no longer lived a life that was in keeping with the standards of the family? What would you lose if you no longer hated your life? What would you gain?

Would you no longer get attention from your mother, who is prone to ignoring you unless you are in some sort of crisis that she can rescue you from?

If you lost the weight you have been wanting to lose, would you also lose all of your hard-earned money because you will have to go out and buy a whole new wardrobe?

What keeps you stuck?

What benefits do you get from staying stuck?

What will you lose if you are no longer stuck?

## Things to Think About

People carry resentment around like a cherished toy. If you break the word "resentment" down into syllables, it looks like "re-sent-ment." Essentially, resentment means *I re-sent it*, as the incident you're upset about goes around and around in your mind and you stew over it. You keep resending it to your psyche to cause more and more damage. You need to release your resentment altogether. Each day is a new day.

An attitude of gratitude can really help you. Just look at the things you have and the wins you have already achieved.

I suggest you get a notebook and keep it by the side of your bed. Every morning before you get up, write down a few of the good things that have happened to you from birth until the present. You can break it down into years, or just write the good things that randomly come to mind. Each night, write down all of the good things that have happened to you during the day.

This is a good tool to take with you when you are having a conversation with the mirror, in case you have forgotten about your wins. Read your list and praise yourself for all the good things you have accomplished. Look at all of the blessings you have been given in your life. Count every good thing, no matter how small.

On the bad days, reading over your list can be a great natural antidepressant.

As you make it a habit, your wins notebook will get bigger and bigger, and soon you will have to get another one—because we all have something good to claim as a win every day.

I was fairly young when I went through my first difficult divorce. It was not a pleasant experience, and I felt like the weight of the world was on my shoulders. One day, I was driving home from work and feeling completely overwhelmed.

As I was barreling down the road, I just happened to notice an incredibly beautiful field full of flowers, and I thought for just a brief moment, *Oh! Look at that! Where did they come from? They weren't there this morning. I need to stop.*

Then my other voice, the snarky one in the back of my head said, *You can't stop! You have to get home. You have work to do.* So I drove further down the road.

Then my reasonable voice spoke up, *You're not going to lose anything if you stop for a minute.* So I stopped, turned around, and went back to the field. I got out of the car and I was amazed. How had that field become so completely covered in blooms since the morning?

I went out into the middle of the field and, after looking around to make sure nobody could observe me, I lay down. All of the flowers were just tall enough to completely cover me. I could hear the bees ecstatically buzzing around and feeding off the flowers.

I looked up at the sky, which was a gorgeous color of blue with white fluffy clouds gently floating across it. There was a small breeze that blew across the tops of the flowers, and their delicate scents wafted over me.

As I lay there, I began to cry. With my tears, every single ounce of pain was washed away. At that moment, it seemed all was right in the world, and those busy little bees were going to take care of everything. I stayed and had a good cry for about 20 minutes. I was grateful for how much better I felt. Then I got up, went back to my car, and continued on my way home.

Even though it happened 30 years ago, that day was a win for me. I think about it often. This blessing, in just a brief moment, came when it seemed nothing was going right in my life.

If you look hard enough, I know you will find something in your life that is going right for you. Maybe it is the hug of a child, maybe it is the smile of a stranger, or maybe it is a compliment from a friend. Some days, it feels like you have to move mountains to find the blessings, but I promise that if you look hard enough, you will find one thing that you can count as good, every single day.

CHAPTER ELEVEN

# Who Are You, Really?
*Live Your Own Life*

> To be yourself in a world that is constantly trying to make you something else is the greatest accomplishment.
>
> —*Ralph Waldo Emerson*

## Life According to Your Authorities

What did your authorities write on your wall about what you should do or be when you grew up? I really wanted to be an airline stewardess, but I was told that if I was traveling all the time, I would not be able to properly take care of my husband and my children.

Next, I wanted to be a model, but it was pointed out to me again—how would I have a family? How would I take care of them if I were modeling? Besides, I was too smart and should use my brain, not my body.

I wanted to be a forest ranger, but girls didn't do this kind of things when I was growing up. It was stressed again and again that my only job and responsibility in life was to be a wife and mother.

I wanted to go to college. I wanted to get a degree. I remember one day when I was in sixth grade. I was enthusiastically talking about what I wanted to be when I grew up and which college I wanted to go to. My father laughed and said, "Girls don't go to college. Your job is to stay home and take care of your husband and raise your children."

I was crushed. I felt as though my father had taken the bright light of my dreams and snuffed them out like a candle. I did not like this answer then and I certainly do not like it now. At some point, a woman is no longer capable of bearing children. Then what? You just stay home and take care of the house? How boring! What if you get a divorce, if you never marry, or if your husband loses his job? What would be your "purpose" then? What about *your* dreams?

On the other hand, if what you want most in life is to be a stay-at-home wife and mother—and that's what you are because you *choose* to be—then consider yourself a successful woman and don't let anyone tell you that you're not. I chose to stay at home with my children and ran successful businesses from my home at the same time. This is what worked for me.

The issue is not about being a stay-at-home mom versus being a career woman. The issue is this: Are you living your life in a way you *choose* because it brings you joy, or are you living according to what someone else said you should do?

Today, girls can grow up to be just about anything they want to be. There are still some very real wage inequality issues, but as a general rule the working world has opened up.

Have you achieved your dreams? Did you become who you wanted to be? Are you in the type of career you wanted to have, or are you doing what everyone else wanted you to do?

There was once a doctor who, as a child, wanted more than anything to be a car mechanic, but his mother did not approve of such a "menial" job. She insisted he had to go to school and become someone of "value"—someone his mother felt could do some good in the world. So, for his mother, he became a doctor.

Instead of repairing cars, he repaired people. Yet, in his heart he wanted more than anything in the world to be a car mechanic.

What do you remember wanting to be when you were a child?

## The Massive Disconnect

So many people are trying to be something or someone they are not.

A president of a major university said that the professional women on her staff were trying so hard to be perfectly efficient that they had lost their true identities. They were out of touch with themselves. Women are no longer allowed to be feminine. They must be aggressive and efficient, and they must be just as good as any man in any career they choose. Men are no longer allowed to be masculine. They are either expected to exhibit gentle, tender, feminine tendencies or macho tendencies, but there does not seem to be room for them to have a bit of both worlds.

We have become disconnected from our passions. We are living on autopilot with somebody else putting in the coordinates.

We are disconnected from our bodies. We live in the ivory towers of our minds and never listen our bodies. Our bodies give us feedback that we ignore, waiting until the last moment to pay attention and provide the help our body has been asking for. By then it is often too late, and disease has a hold on us.

We have disconnected from being kind—to ourselves and to each other. If you said the things to a friend that you say to yourself, would you have any friends?

We have disconnected from the environment. We have disconnected from the results of our actions on the environment around us. As a result, we have global climate change and many other environmental disasters that are the result of the pursuit of power and money instead of caring about the greater good for all.

We have disconnected from humanity. We live vicariously by avidly following reality TV stars and other public figures, and we know more about their day-to-day lives than those of our own family members. We watch the news and learn about the horrific things that are being done to other people, but we feel nothing and we do nothing about it.

In the interest of reconnecting with yourself, what are *your* passions? What did you want to be when you grew up? If money were no object, what would you really like to do with your time?

What makes your heart sing? Write down the things that bring you joy. How often do you do the things you love?

One of the things that brings me joy is teaching. I feel such joy when watching people get the "Aha" behind a concept they finally understand. I particularly enjoy teaching women how to overcome their limiting beliefs and traumatic pasts, and reach for their dreams, achieve them, and change their lives. This is my passion. It is what brings me joy, but it took me a long time to get here.

## What Have You Done with Your Dreams?

Write down the things that make you happy and bring you joy. How often do you participate in doing these things? When was the last time you learned something new that you enjoy? If you are not learning and growing, you are stagnating and dying.

Too often, fear holds us back. Fear simply means "False Evidence Appearing Real." We work ourselves up into a frenzy worrying about things that haven't even happened yet. If something negative has happened, we worry about all the other things that could go wrong—the majority of which haven't even happened, and most likely won't. Yet worrying about something imagined can give a person an ulcer.

When was the last time you took a chance and did something that took you outside of your comfort zone? It might be a new activity; it might be taking up dancing or bicycle riding or a sport you really enjoy but thought you would never be able to do.

I recently taught a class of senior citizens. The majority of participants in the class were excited by the idea that they weren't done living yet—that they were still alive and they still had dreams that could be achieved. The oldest person in the class was 86!

I reminded the participants that age is a state of mind and that they could reawaken their dreams. Some of the ideas we discussed were having a house on the beach, traveling the world, starting a new business, making more money, writing a book, or learning how to play a new instrument.

One of the participants kept adamantly saying, "The examples you are giving are not reasonable for a senior citizen to achieve." For the entire six weeks I taught the class, this woman kept insisting that having a big dream was not a reasonable goal for a senior citizen. Why not? Why should there be an age limit on dreams?

I never did change her mind—she is the only one who can do that. Yet the other participants happily created goals for the golden years of their lives, however long their lives might be. Waking up in the morning saying, "Well, I'm still here!" and working toward their goals was invigorating for many of them.

One of my goals is to hike to the top of Mt. Denali on my 90th birthday. Someone asked me why I was going to wait until I was 90; why didn't I do it now, when I'm young? My reply was that I want to have the kind of stamina and health needed to hike a mountain when I am 90 years old. Meanwhile, I will have to practice and work up to this height on other mountains, which will keep me in very good physical condition.

What kind of dreams have you put on hold? Who says you cannot accomplish them? Is it a conversation you are having with yourself, or is it something on your wall—a belief that somebody inscribed a long time ago that said, *This is what you need to become* and *this is how you should behave.*

Many years ago, I was very interested in my Native American ancestors and their culture. I wanted a beautiful buckskin dress. When I told my mother, she said, "When are you ever going to grow up and stop being such a hippie?"

I felt shame when she accused me of being a hippie. Why should I feel shame? I'm proud of my Native American heritage; yet exploring it was not acceptable to her. I can only guess what her problem was, but her disapproval successfully stopped me from continuing that line of study for a time.

Think about the kinds of things people say to you that keep you from accomplishing your dreams.

When I was a young woman, I was engaged to marry a young man I'll call Kyle. He was nearly perfect. Kyle was kind, gentle, enthusiastic, and ambitious. He had an adventurous, mischievous nature, yet my brothers did not approve of him because he was always courteous and would ask my opinion. My brothers felt that a real man made his own decisions and his own rules, and did not bother to ask a woman's opinion. If a woman cried, a real man should just slap her until she stopped being "hysterical." There were many times when my brothers put Kyle down because, in their opinion, he didn't measure up to some obscure expectations.

One of the things inscribed on my wall is the importance of having your father approve of the young man you are about to marry. I had broken off contact with my father, and I was not about to ask his blessing on my marriage to Kyle. I felt that my brothers would be good stand-ins for my father, but I knew they didn't approve. However, there was another guy of whom they did approve, and they constantly suggested that I would be better off if I were married to him.

I had so many misconceptions about what being married really meant. I had been taught that sexual attraction and passion was a sin, and that I should submit to my husband in all things. I was not sexually attracted to the man my family wanted me to marry. Somewhere in my confused mind I thought this was a good thing—as if babies showed up from doing dishes or vacuuming.

Against my own heart and my desires, I broke off my engagement with Kyle and married the man my brothers approved of. The social pressure was intense. My mother had spent all the money on the cake and decorations, and family members had traveled for miles to attend. Wedding gifts had been arriving for days. How could I possibly change my mind? What would people think of me?

On the day of the wedding, I remember feeling like part of me was locked inside a nightmarish soundproof room, screaming, *No! Don't do this*! I felt completely trapped and powerless as I dissociated my mind from my body and moved through the day, smiling and responding the way I was expected to. I will never forget the feeling of hopelessness that descended on me when I whispered, "I do." The tears I wept were not tears of joy. I knew I had made the biggest mistake of my life, but I felt as if the doors of doom had sealed me in the marriage forever. I felt as though heavy doors and shuttered windows closed all the light out of my life and all I could see was darkness. I knew my family would not rescue me, and I did not know how to rescue myself.

My new husband continued the cycle of abuse I had grown up with, and I submitted to it because it was what I was used to.

Somehow, deep in my heart, I did not believe I deserved kindness and love from someone who respected me. After all, I had never known anything else. I experienced two failed marriages before I found someone who was kind and loving.

I married my first husband for my family, my second husband for the sake of my children, and my third husband just for myself.

When I first started dating Jeffrey, I did not tell anyone in my family of origin about him. By the time we agreed to marry,

I had decided I didn't care whether my family approved of him or not. *I loved him*, he was a good man, and my children loved him. This was all that mattered. Quite frankly, my family did not approve of him, but we have been married for over 21 years now and he is my best friend.

Who are you in a relationship with? Is it someone you chose to be with, or are you in a relationship with someone your family approves of and they chose for you?

I know I am not the only person who has married someone because they felt they had to. I have heard this same kind of story from other women. Perhaps your family expects you to marry the guy you have been dating for years, but when it comes right down to it you don't want to. Going through with it anyway never turns out good. I have never heard anyone say, "Oh, I was wrong; it turned out so much better than I thought it would."

When my children got married, I made sure they knew it was okay for them to say "No" if they wanted to. I didn't care how much money I had spent on the wedding, I did not want them to repeat my mistake. I wanted to make certain they were not choosing their life partner based on some erroneous inscription on their walls.

This works in all aspects of our lives. How we choose where to work and whom we interact with is all based on our walls. Once upon a time, you dreamed about what your life would be like. You imagined what kind of a house you would live in, what your future companion would look like, and what you would do with your day. What happened to these dreams?

I remember being told that boys do not wear pink and girls do not wear blue. Blue is my favorite color. I happen to look very lovely in blue, and I have seen some guys who can really rock pink.

What kinds of beliefs do you have that do not serve you anymore?

## Reawakening Your Dreams

Write down everything you would love to do but haven't done before, whether it is traveling to Paris, bungee jumping off a really high bridge, parasailing, starting your own company, or joining the Peace Corps—anything you feel that nobody else would approve of but in your heart you really want to do. Imagine there are no limits to your dreams. You have all the time and money in the world. What would you love to do?

Write these things down and review your list. Dare to dream your dreams. Dare to live your own life. Dare to accept 100% Responsibility and take control of your own life.

You can choose whether or not to allow somebody else to control your life. You choose whether or not to pursue your dreams—these are choices. Choosing not to make a decision is still a decision.

You might say, "Oh, but I don't have the money." If it is something you really truly want, you will find the money. How many of us have purchased something we "did not have the money for" but we really wanted? If there is something you really want to do—and you have written it down on your list—then I say go for it and discover the joy of living your own life.

CHAPTER TWELVE

# Forgiveness and the Parable of the Horses

> **Definition of Forgiveness:** "Forgiveness is the intentional and voluntary process by which a victim undergoes a change in feelings and attitude regarding an offense; lets go of negative emotions, such as vengefulness, with an increased ability to wish the offender well."
>
> —Wikipedia.com

## Forgiveness is a Process

In order to heal from the traumas of your past, it is imperative to forgive everyone involved, including yourself. This can be very difficult, but the quality of the rest of your life depends on your willingness to forgive. Although forgiveness is a *choice*, it is also a *process*.

Passions are strong emotions. I do not advocate acting on negative emotions, but merely validating them. When we admit, *Oh, I am angry* or *Wow, I feel humiliated* or *Gee, I really don't like that person*, we will be able to look at our emotions objectively and choose to express them or not.

It is empowering to acknowledge and validate our emotions. It enables us to choose our responses rather than stuffing the emotion and denying its existence, leaving the invalidated emotion to wreak havoc with our spiritual, mental, emotional, and physical body.

We were given our emotions when we were created. They are part of the human makeup. Everybody has them. To say that emotions are evil or bad is to say that a part of every single one of us is intrinsically evil. We are put here on earth to learn to discipline ourselves, to prove whether or not we can be valiant in keeping the commandments of God.

Part of learning to discipline ourselves is to gain mastery over our emotions. We have negative and positive emotions. Some of them make us feel good; some make us feel bad; some engender harmony with our fellow travelers on this mortal plane, and some cause strife and disharmony. Some emotions draw us near to God, and some drive us away from Him.

Negative emotions, such as hate, fear, anger, and shame, do not feel good to us or the people around us—unless they are cruel and enjoy that sort of thing, which is a whole different issue. What our negative emotions try to do, however, is protect us.

For example, the fear of public speaking is one of the most common fears that people face. If someone laughed at us when we had to give a talk at the front of the classroom when we were nine years old, we probably felt shame or humiliation. Our subconscious, which is also our protector, will do its level best to never let us get in any situation again where we MIGHT feel the same painful emotions. We will either be completely unable to speak in public, or we will break out in a sweat and feel terribly uncomfortable every time we try.

There is a difference between expressing our emotions and validating them. To express an emotion is to make a choice to let it spill out of the confines of our own mental and physical space and invade the spaces of everyone close to us. This is not necessarily a bad thing—it depends on which emotion we choose to express and whether or not we validate and release it.

If we throw a terrible temper tantrum in the privacy of a deep, dark forest with no living person around us and we feel better, let it go, and are able to return to our families in a cheerful, peaceful mood, then it is beneficial.

However, if we throw the same tantrum, get in our car, and drive home while fuming and chewing over whatever upset us—and upon arriving home we swallow our raging emotion and paste a false smile on our faces—we have done ourselves and everyone we come in contact with a terrible harm.

It is even worse if we do not swallow our raging emotion, but instead throw it (now in its festering acidic form) all over our family members or coworkers.

Conversely, most people do not object when love and joy spill over into their personal space. These emotions are positive, giving emotions. Unfortunately, some people have become so expert at stuffing their emotions that they are unable to express either their positive *or* negative emotions, or perhaps they have dulled themselves with addictions and don't know what they feel.

To illustrate this principle, let us explore what I call the "Parable of the Horses." In the *Book of Mormon*, Alma 38:12, it reads:

> "Use boldness but not overbearance and also see that you bridle all your passions that you may be filled with love. . . ."

In this parable, the horses represent our emotions and the stable represents the human soul, mind, and body. When we bridle our passions, our emotions, it is like bridling a horse. We put a bridle on a horse so we can train it, guide it, and direct it, and, when necessary, control it.

The same principle works with our emotions. If we stuff our feelings and deny that we have them, it is like standing in a stable full of lively horses and saying, "There are no horses here." In order to master something, you have to understand and acknowledge it.

In order to control the horse named "Anger," for example, it is important to understand why the horse is agitated. Is the Anger horse trying to protect you, or is it reminding you of something bad that happened to you as a child. Does the Anger horse feel you are in a similarly dangerous situation again and it needs to protect you?

The Anger horse can be dangerous. Many people say, "Just trot out the Forgiveness horse and lock that nasty Anger horse back in his stall." This, however, does not train or appease the Anger horse, which is still desperately trying to protect you. Perhaps in an effort to get its message across to you, the Anger horse will kick down the walls of the stall, which could manifest in your life as physical, mental, or emotional illness.

## Steps to Forgiveness

Forgiveness is a conscious choice, and there are actual steps that must be followed in order to complete the process. We talk about forgiving all the time, but we never talk about the process.

Some things are relatively easy to forgive. If you come home after being gone longer than you anticipated and discover that your dog had an "accident" on the floor, you will most likely grumble, clean up the mess, and forgive your dog. If your toddler spills milk all over the freshly mopped kitchen floor, you might cry, but you clean it up and forgive your toddler. The size of these transgressions seems relatively small and forgiveness comes without much effort.

Other things are very difficult to forgive, such as betrayal, infidelity, theft, murder, or any of the myriad horrible things people do to one another. These can be forgiven, too, as we witnessed in the example of the Amish community in Philadelphia, when an angry milk truck driver murdered five of their precious daughters. The forgiveness and charity they showed the family of the murderer is exemplary.

When a 17-year-old drunken boy crashed his vehicle into Chris Williams' car and killed Chris' wife, unborn child, and two children, Chris chose to forgive. His choice changed his life, the life of the young man who hit them, and the entire community.

There are many examples of forgiveness being offered every day. Forgiveness is a transforming choice and completely necessary for your healing. If you cannot forgive the people who have hurt you, you cannot heal completely.

Do not compare your process to someone else's. If it takes you a while longer to forgive someone—this is your process—cut yourself some slack. Don't compare yourself to the people in the examples I have given. The speeds of their forgiveness are exceptions rather than rules—it is something we can aspire to as we grow into better people. However, you *can* choose how quickly you progress through the steps. You have this power.

The steps are:

- Recognize that you are having difficulty forgiving someone. Acknowledge that they have offended you, or upset or hurt you in some way. At this point, there is a choice. Do you choose to stuff your emotions, or do you choose to process them? Hopefully, you choose to process them so they don't become toxic in your body.
- Invite God or your higher power to help you overcome your negative emotions and forgive others. Again, make the conscious choice to process your emotions.
- Admit and acknowledge all your feelings about the problem. What are your true feelings about the person involved? What are your true feelings about the situation? What are your true feelings regarding the consequences you know about so far? As you know, consequences often go beyond what we can see.
- Have a conversation with a chair. We talked about this in Chapter 7. You put a picture on the chair (if you have a

picture of the troubling individual) and then you tell off the chair. You tell the chair all of the things that you would like to say to the person who has offended or hurt you. If you are angry and you usually yell when you are angry, then yell, holler. If you usually throw or hit things, take a towel and hit the chair or throw the towel at the chair. Get it all out. Repeat this as often as necessary until you begin to feel peaceful.

- Every time you think a negative thought about the person, say "Cancel! Cancel!" and replace it with a loving thought.
- Choose to let it go. This must be a conscious choice. You must actually say out loud, "I choose to forgive (person's name)." It might be necessary to say it more than once, but it must be a conscious choice. Otherwise, if you just say *whatever*, then you are simply stuffing the emotion again.

## Holding on to Negative Emotions

Our emotional makeup is very much like a bubbling tar barrel. The barrel is full of all the traumas we have experienced in our past, as well as those we experience currently. Memories bubble to the surface of our consciousness in random order. One moment, something from age 3 might surface, and the next memory could be something from age 11.

What happens to your body when you hold on to your negative emotions? They will get trapped in a weak area of your body. If you have been sexually abused, they will most likely lodge in the reproductive organs. If you are harboring hatred for someone, it will most often lodge in your colon.

Karol Truman has developed a protocol for how emotions affect our physical body. In her book *Feelings Buried Alive Never Die*, you can look up almost any illness you might be having. Next to each illness there is a list of the possible feelings that go along with the problem. For example, if you are having a pain in your shoulder and it hurts really bad, one of the things listed for this type of pain is *bearing burdens that are not yours to bear*. It's amazing how accurate these illness lists are.

What happens to your soul when you hold on to negative emotions? They are very much like acid, and they will canker and destroy all the goodness and light in your nature, and you will become bitter and cantankerous and unforgiving. It is like shriveling inside yourself, dying while still breathing and walking around.

When you poke an amoeba with a pin, it flinches inwards. It does not expand itself outwards and say, *Wow, that was fun; let's do it again*. Instead, it flinches in on itself.

Every time a person hold onto a negative emotion, their psyche flinches just like poking an amoeba with a pin. The more a person stuffs their negative emotions, the less open their psyche will be. They begin to shrink in on themselves. They draw darkness around themselves like a cold blanket; they do not open up and allow the world in.

Is this the kind of life you desire, or would you prefer to let the negative emotions go and have light and joy, happiness and love in your life?

## Tools for Your Journey to Soul Shift™

You can use the chair exercise to process your feelings. Another good exercise is to write down all your negative emotions about someone or something on little slips of paper. Put the paper inside a very special bowl that you choose just for this purpose and set them on fire. Imagine that as the smoke rises into the air, the negative energy dissipates, too.

CHAPTER THIRTEEN

# The Desires of Your Heart

**Definition of Desire:** "A conscious impulse toward something that promises enjoyment or satisfaction in its attainment."

—merriam-webster.com

## Own Your Dreams

The biggest battle we will ever wage and the greatest trial we will ever face goes on daily between our own ears and within our own hearts. How we think and feel about ourselves or our experiences, other people, and our God determines whether we will find joy in our day or be overburdened by our experiences.

We really can do anything we want to do, within reason. Of course, we can't change our skin color, fly without wings, or add or subtract inches to our height, but most of the things we really want to do, we can accomplish.

There are four types of dreams:

- Discarded dreams
- Outgrown dreams
- Evergreen dreams
- New dreams

Discarded dreams are dreams we have given up and thrown to the side because we do not see any way they can ever come true. This might include dreams of a nice house, a different car, a different style of clothing, a happy relationship—all of the dreams we feel will never come to pass because they have not happened yet. We discard them, thinking, *My life is always going to be like this—this is just the way it is.* When a person discards their dreams just because they can't see them ever coming to pass, they throw out hope and make room for despair.

Outgrown dreams are dreams that no longer interest us. Our life has taken a different direction, perhaps, or we realize it was not reasonable for us to want to be a dragon, or whatever. When you believe you have outgrown a dream, check to make sure you have not outgrown it because you think you are too old. Age should have nothing to do with it. If you have kept yourself in good health and vitality, then why not go after your dreams? If you realize the dream would be possible if you were healthier, then make regaining your health and vitality a goal so you can achieve your dreams. There are plenty of inspirational stories of people who ran their first marathon at age 60, or even older.

Evergreen dreams are the ones you keep forever. When you think about what your life will be like in five years, you still feel you really would love to do them. Looking back over your life, you know it's the same dream you had when you were 5 or 20, or whatever age you might have first dreamed it.

When you have an evergreen dream, you continually carry the hope in your heart that somehow it will come to pass. These are dreams that have not changed because your circumstances have changed, your interests have changed, or you have changed as a person. They are dreams that you carry in your heart because they are your true desires.

The fourth type of dream is a *new* dream. These are dreams that come because of new opportunities or other changes in our lives.

Being a speaker, facilitator, and trainer was not something I envisioned doing when I was in my 20s, but now it is definitely my passion to be an international speaker and empower women throughout the world to reach their dreams.

Would you love to learn to play the piano, or are you only in love with the *idea* of playing the piano? Would you really love to live a different kind of life, or are you only in love with the *idea* of having a different life? Would you love to learn to fly, or are you in love with the *idea* of flying? Would you love to run your own business, or are you only in love with talking and dreaming about it?

Many people become caught up with the "if only" that prevents them from achieving their dreams. When the opportunity to create positive change shows up, they hesitate to grasp the "bull by the horns" and take charge of their experience. Life is full of missed and unseen opportunities.

Many people whisper a quiet requiem for their dreams, telling themselves, *If only I had been born into a different family. If only my parents had let me be an exchange student. If only I had more money. If only my circumstances were different. If only I had children. If only I did not have children. If only I had married someone else.*

"If only" is closely intertwined with "I'll be happy when." *I'll be happy when I get married. I'll be happy when I get divorced. I'll be happy when I have children. I'll be happy when my kids are grown. I'll be happy when I get to take a trip to [wherever]. I'll be happy when I no longer have this job. I'll be happy when I get that raise. I'll be happy when I retire.*

Life goes on and sometimes things happen unexpectedly. Opportunities align in such a way that you really can pursue your dreams. You get what you focus on. If you focus on making your dream a reality, your brain works to make sure it comes to pass. When you focus on a goal, you begin to notice things you didn't notice before. You'll meet people who can help you get closer to your goal, people you would not have met under any other circumstances. Many of these things might seem coincidental, but they are the result of focus and the universe conspiring to do you good.

When all of your excuses evaporate, do you find yourself backing away and telling yourself, *Oh my heavens, now I have to do something about that dream.*

Recently, I was shocked and chagrined to discover something about myself. For several years, I had been saying that I wanted to start my own business being a professional speaker and transformational life coach; however, there were two enormous obstacles to this plan.

Number one was the money. There was never any money. Being self-employed and working on commission only, there was never a steady paycheck to count on and budgeting was tough. Every penny counted. My son, who is a weight-lifter, was growing so fast it seemed that he needed new clothes every week, and his appetite was astonishing!

Just when it seemed like maybe we would have a little money to put aside, something unpleasant and unexpected would come up, like the car needing new tires, the taxes were due, one of our older children needed financial help, or the computer gave up the ghost.

My second excuse was that I was a full-time caregiver for my mother, who suffered from dementia and lived with us. I was sure she had somehow discovered the secret to immortality and I would be caring for her forever. Her care schedule was so demanding and inflexible that I knew I would never have time to start my own business.

Nevertheless, I designed my dream business. I talked about it in loving detail. I described every nuance of the business to my long-suffering husband. I fiddled with logos and details of the program. I dreamed of the retreat facility I would have and spent hours longingly looking at real estate online to find the perfect place, yet I felt so trapped that I could not go look at any of the places I found.

I listened to every free business webinar I could find and planned for the day when I would be able to take the courses necessary to teach me the ins and outs of running a business structured like the one I dreamed about.

I investigated software companies in my field to be sure I knew which company I wanted to go with when I could finally afford them. I fretted that someone else might pluck my idea out of my head and do it sooner than I could, and that by the time I got around to it my great idea would belong to someone else.

I threw temper tantrums and wept with frustration, believing it was never going to happen. I was convinced that I would be ancient and crusty by the time things came together and I might actually have the time and resources to begin.

Then something miraculous happened. I was clearing up some clutter in my home. I went through the garage and closets, and decided that if I hadn't touched an item in a year I didn't really need it. Various items I had been hanging on to forever went to auction. Almost simultaneously, my caregiving responsibilities shifted. In a short period of time, I had some unexpected money that was not pegged for anything else and I had extra time.

At first, I was elated. I talked more about what I was going to do and how excited I was to do it. I had the software websites I had decided to go with pulled up on my computer, but I was sure that I needed just a little more investigation to make sure they were the right choice before I invested any money.

It seemed like so many little things had to be done before I could really get started, and I could not figure out the sequencing. I spun in circles trying to figure out the perfect way to approach all the tasks I needed to accomplish.

Since I am a transformation coach, I cannot hide things from myself, at least not for very long. I try, but I am really good at what I do, and I can see right through myself most of the time.

While staring at my computer screen one day, I realized that I was afraid—not simply afraid but paralyzed. When I really paid attention, I realized I was trembling deep inside. I had been talking about starting this business for so long—but with the comforting and safe idea in the back of my head that it would never happen. After all, I would probably never have enough money and my mother was going to live forever—but things had changed.

My mother still might live forever, but now I had to step out of my comfort zone and do something with my dream or shut up about it. I had to actually do the work to make the business a reality. Was I willing to do whatever was needed, or did I just want to continue dreaming about having a different life?

At some point, you have to do the work that allows you to achieve whatever it is you really would love to do. There's an old adage that says, "Work is just opportunity in disguise." I had to roll up my sleeves and get to work, because nobody else but me could make my dream come to pass.

For years, I said that I would love to learn to play an instrument, such as the harp or the cello. There was always an excuse. At first, I was raising kids in a one-income household; then we had several years of severe financial setbacks; and then mom moved in with us.

One day, I admitted to myself that I probably will never learn to play either instrument because even though I took harp lessons, I did not really make the effort to learn. It is one of those "I would really love to," but what I really mean is "I really love the *idea* of playing the cello or the harp" or "I really love to listen to someone else play" these instruments. It is so easy to blame others for our failed dreams.

I never took instrument lessons as a kid because my parents would not let me take band—so what stopped me from taking some kind of instrument lessons when I grew up? The thing that stopped me was I did not have the true, compelling desire to do anything about it. The things we really have the desire to do, we manage to do.

When I was a child, it was really important to learn how to ride a bike, even though I did not have one of my own. I borrowed one and learned how to ride in one day. Later in life, I really wanted to go to Hawaii—I have traveled there twice.

I have always been drawn to herbal medicine and I wanted to attend the best herbal college I could find. I managed to do this, too, and I graduated with a Master Herbalist degree from the School of Natural Healing while my youngest son was still small.

My family and I envisioned a beautiful home where a 98-year-old wreck of a building stood, and we managed to restore it and transform it into something gorgeous with determination and lots of blood, sweat, and tears.

The most dangerous words anyone ever uses with me are the words, "You can't." I see these words as a challenge, and heaven help anyone who gets in my way. Sometimes, these words even transform something I did not really have any deep desire to accomplish into a passion that will not be denied.

There is something powerful about the emotion that gets behind whatever it is you are attempting to accomplish or whatever you dream of doing. If you are just dreaming because it is pleasant, then enjoy the dream, but you have to accept responsibility for your choice. You cannot blame anyone else when your dream does not come to fruition.

There is a story I heard many years ago about a young man who went to visit a wise old man because he had the desire to be as wise and knowledgeable as the older man. The Ancient man took the young man down to the seashore. Without a word, he waded into the water.

When he was about waist deep, he turned and gestured to the young man to join him. Puzzled, the young man waded out into the water. When he reached the wise man's side, the old man grabbed him by the back of the neck and forced his head under the water.

Struggling, the young man fought to get his head above the water, but the old man was surprisingly strong and kept him under. When the young man's struggles began to weaken, the wise old man pulled him up out of the water and dragged him to the shore. He waited as the young man lay gasping on the sand and then he spoke:

"When you want knowledge and wisdom as much as you wanted that next breath of air, I will be willing to teach you."

Then the wise old man turned around and returned to his home.

When we really want to make changes in our lives, we are propelled toward our goal by:

> *Determination* in the face of failure or seemingly insurmountable obstacles,
> The *belief* that we can achieve the change we desire, and
> The *pleasure* and *satisfaction* we know we will feel when we have achieved it.

There will be choices all along the way as you progress toward your goal. When I set a goal for myself, I always make sure I add, *If not this, then something better.* This allows for little course corrections towards fulfilling the kind of life you really want to have. It also acknowledges that God is in charge, and you are flexible enough to work with Him to find peace and joy.

If you're ready to achieve a Soul Shift, it is time to do some housecleaning.

Go through your list of dreams. It helps to take time to write them all out. Really think about what you would love to do or have—whatever your dream is—and whether you are merely in love with the idea of doing or having whatever it is. Be completely honest with yourself. Is it your dream, or someone else's dream for you?

If you discover after serious reflection that it is only a pleasurable fantasy, move it to your mental entertainment file and cross it off your list of things you want to do. Then concentrate on the things that truly are the desires of your heart. Take 100% Responsibility for achieving your dreams, share your dreams with other people, take action, and have fun!

## Dare to Dream—Live Your Dreams

My dream of being an international speaker and trainer is unfolding. I am still working toward having a resort where clients can come and be empowered to release their negative emotions and limiting beliefs in a safe and loving environment. They will learn how to craft their dreams and begin anew to achieve them.

My life is so much different than anything I could have imagined many years ago. When I started on my path to be a speaker and trainer, I could not see any end results. I could not even see a few feet in front of me, but I took the step and made the effort. By virtue of doing this, everything I need has been drawn to me.

I have met amazing people I had no idea even existed, and I get to develop partnerships with them. God, or the Universe, whatever you want to call it, looks out for me. My life is full and rich, and I find so much joy and peace in everything I do.

There are many dreams I still have yet to realize, but I know they will come to pass because, so far, all of the goals I have put my mind to have come to pass.

What is the one dream you would like to achieve? Start with one. What would it look like? Write in detail about what your life will be like when you have achieved your dream. Act as if you have already achieved it and you will be amazed by what can happen.

CHAPTER FOURTEEN

# As a Man (or a Woman) Thinketh

Proverbs 23:7: "For as he thinketh in his heart, so is he."

—Holy Bible, King James Version

"Much more surprising things can happen to anyone who, when a disagreeable or discouraged thought comes into his mind, just has the sense to remember in time and push it out by putting in an agreeable, determinedly courageous one, two things cannot be in one place."

—*Francis Hodgson Burnett,* The Secret Garden

## The Heart versus the Head

When we are conceived, the organs that form first are the bowel, the heart, and the brain. They all develop from the same clump of embryonic tissue. When this piece of tissue divides, one piece grows into your brain and cranial nerves, or central nervous system, and the other section becomes your enteric nervous system, or "gut-brain." Later on, these two sections are connected by a huge nerve called the "vagus nerve."

Understanding this connection helps explain why, when your thinking brain panics and says, *I have got to give a speech in front of how many people?* your stomach begins to do flip-flops, or you might have to rush to the bathroom.

The heart is connected to the brain with the same kinds of tissues. This explains why the proverb says *thinketh in his heart* instead of simply *thinketh* or *thinketh in his head*. The heart forms and begins beating 22 days after conception.

Researchers at the Association for Prenatal and Perinatal Psychology and Health have studied and proven scientifically that the fetus, or embryo of the child, is responsive to the emotions and thoughts of the mother. This is why when a mother does not want the child, the child knows it, and this is imprinted in the child's cellular system.

What you think about becomes your reality. Thinking determines your emotions—not the other way around. Words like "hate," "war," "anger," and "fear" fill the body, mind, and soul with darkness. The words "love," "happiness," "joy," and "peace" fill the body, mind, and soul with light. The more you think positive thoughts, the more light you will find within.

This can be demonstrated by using kinesiology. Kinesiology is a method of muscle testing that can be used to find out what your body really feels about something.

Imagine you are standing in front of a crowded room with your eyes closed. If I asked the people in the audience to think negative, ugly thoughts about you, your body would begin to lean backwards, because your body and psyche would recoil from the negative energy. The first time I watched this happen, I was amazed. I thought it was a trick, but I have witnessed this many times with different people and it always works.

This is what we do when something is unpleasant and negative. We don't rush towards it; we try to get away from it, which is why our body leans away.

If I ask the audience to project loving, kind thoughts, you will begin to lean towards the audience, because when we feel love and kindness and generosity, which are good and giving feelings, we lean into them. Even with our eyes closed and without the visual cues of body language or facial expression we are able to feel the positive energy of the audience.

If you walk into a room full of people, you can tell immediately when somebody is really angry, because you will pick up on the vibrations the person is putting out.

What you think about becomes your reality. In 1903, James Allen wrote a book titled *As a Man Thinketh*. He wrote this important truth in the Foreword when he described the purpose of his book. He said:

> ". . . its object being to stimulate men and women to the discovery and perception of the truth that they themselves are makers of themselves by virtue of the thoughts which they choose and encourage, that mind is the master weaver both of the inner garment of character and the outer garment of circumstance and that as they may have hitherto woven in ignorance and pain, they may now weave in enlightenment and happiness."

*As A Man Thinketh* is now in the public domain and it can be downloaded from the Internet.

I was at a conference in California recently. Before I left, I stopped in front of a note on my office door that says, "Success Leaves Clues." I repeated this phrase to myself several times as a reminder of the reason I was going to the conference.

On the last day of the conference, before the doors were opened, I noticed a gentleman sitting at a table and writing. I make a habit of trying to meet new people every time I go somewhere, so I walked over, introduced myself, and asked him what he was doing.

He showed me some notes he was writing on an anthology in which he had written a chapter; then he shared the chapter with me. As we continued our conversation, I discovered that we knew some of the same people, and I was impressed that success was something he was very interested in.

As the conversation went on, he told me that, yes, he had written a few other books, and he was working on a chapter for another anthology that was going to be published by the same men who had done the first anthology. He also explained that he had written a book of his own. He pulled out a brochure for me to look at; it showed a picture of him standing, looking very nice on the front of it. His name is Miguel A. de Jesus. "Oh," he said. "I have also written this other book. . . ."

He turned the brochure over and showed me the title of his other book: *Success Leaves Clues*. It was the very book I had been thinking about as I was leaving to go the conference. How did I manage to meet the man who wrote the book? It was because of what I was *thinking* about—because I was interested in it, and his book title was the phrase I kept repeating to myself.

Was it just a coincidence? I have always believed that coincidence is God's way of remaining anonymous, and I believe that I met Miguel A. de Jesus because it was important for me to meet him.

Another story of how what you think about becomes your reality came from my mother. I lived with her for a time in a nice house that had a river rock fireplace. To the side of this fireplace there were two stairs that went down, and there was a little hole right at the base of the second step. I always kept my daughter's shoes tucked away on that step so they would be out of the way and nobody would step on them.

Every time my mother went near the steps, she would pick up the shoes and say, "I hate that hole! I keep thinking a snake is going to come out of it." I lived with my mother for about a year, and every single time she went past the hole she would repeat the same thing.

One day, she screamed at the top of her lungs. I ran into the front room and asked, "Mom, what's wrong?" All the color had drained from her face, and for the first time in her life she was completely speechless. She pointed a shaking finger at the fireplace. I went over cautiously and looked by the fireplace and, sure enough, there was a snake that had come up through the hole.

Someone once said that my mother did not bring the snake to her by thinking about it all the time, but rather it was her premonition about the snake showing up. I disagree with this explanation. I believe my mother thought about the snake coming up through that hole so much that the Universe complied with her wish and delivered the snake to her.

What kind of power does our thinking have? How can we control our world with our thoughts? We can control it by keeping our positive goals and aspirations constantly before us.

## Change Your Thoughts, Change Your World

Many years ago, Dr. Albert Schweitzer, a Nobel Prize winner, was asked his opinion on what was wrong with men. His answer was, "Men simply don't think."

"Of course I think," you object, "I think all the time!"

Yes, but what do you think about?

When life got really hard to deal with, I tried not to think of anything. I put my brain on "hum"—white noise. I would bury myself in a good book and ignore everything and everyone around me by immersing myself in the life of the characters on the page. I would play games on my phone or computer for hours. Television was not one of my addictions, but it easily could have been.

Not thinking is choosing not to change your life. You absolutely have the power to make changes in your circumstances, but not if you choose to avoid thinking about it. Although conscious thinking can change your life, keep in mind that you cannot change another person's behavior.

For example, thinking, *I am in a loving, kind, gentle, compassionate, and passionate relationship* cannot change your significant other, no matter how often you visualize or repeat or think it. Your significant other must decide to make changes on his (or her) own.

What *will* happen, however, is that your behavior will change and your significant other will either change in response to you or because of the changes you have made in yourself, or you will draw to yourself the kind of relationship you would rather be in.

If you are not in a relationship and your affirmation is, *I am in a loving, kind, gentle, compassionate, and passionate relationship,* the intention of your affirmation will draw the perfect person to you.

Most of us have gone through this scenario: we have something we want to change in our lives. We want to be happier. Perhaps it is just that we want to think more positive thoughts. We make a conscious effort to police our thoughts, and whenever we find ourselves thinking negatively we replace these thoughts with positive ones. So far, so good.

We go along in this vein for a while and discover that it really is not easy to think positive thoughts about ourselves because we do not really believe them, anyway. Then we begin to sabotage ourselves again, which seems to prove the whole concept of *as a man thinketh* is nonsense and, by extension, suggests that we are not worthy of whatever goal we desire and that we believe will bring us happiness. The reality is that we must push through the resistance and difficulties to create real, deep, and lasting change.

For many people, changing their habitual thought processes requires a gargantuan effort of sheer will. There are those who are able to make changes in their thought processes by exerting their will. This is when desire and belief come in. Do we really desire with all our hearts to make changes, to think more positively and become happier, and do we believe we are capable of it?

Equally important, do we believe we are worthy of happiness?

The birth of each of my children was a magical, miraculous thing. To know that I, in company with my husband, was blessed to join with God in creating a new life was beyond anything I have ever experienced. Having that new little person placed in my arms for the first time was sacred and I find it difficult to describe.

I held each of my four beautiful children for hours on end, marveling at their tiny noses, those perfect little fingers and toes. I would trace the line of their elf-like ears, caress their soft skin, and play with their impossibly soft hair. I looked into those bright, curious, blue or brown eyes and tried to convey to them somehow that they were perfect and I would always love them.

Looking at a newborn and feeling the heavenly feeling that comes from them, it is impossible to imagine that they are capable of evil . . . and they are not. Not one of us is born evil or bad. A person becomes bad either by training or by choice. Until children are eight years of age, they are not old enough to be accountable for their choices.

The people who raise children can train them, either accidentally or on purpose, to seek out and act out things that are not good, thus setting them on the path to becoming an evil or bad person. However, even in the worst circumstances, never underestimate the power of the soul to be good and overcome environmental factors.

It is important to realize that children who are raised in terrible circumstances can—and do—choose not to embrace the evil around them, and they reach adulthood as good people.

As a natural result of our being intrinsically good by birthright, most of us are muddling along doing the best we can, always in pursuit of that thing we call "happiness." It is important to understand that a Soul Shift can take place in either direction. You can choose to shift toward being a better person, or you can choose to shift toward being a bad person. It's your choice.

However, you must understand that although you might find fleeting pleasure in wickedness, you cannot find happiness. There are laws in our universe that will not be defied, and this is one of them.

Every day before you go to bed, spend five minutes writing down the things you are grateful for. Stretch your mind and try to write something different each day so it does not turn into a laundry list of the same things. It will mean more to you if you really look for things to be grateful for, rather than getting into a rut.

## Goals

We have all had somebody say, "You need to make short-term, mid-term, and long-term goals." We have dutifully written down an idea about something we might want to accomplish in one year, five years, and ten years. Chances are, we have forgotten exactly what we wrote. I used to hate these exercises, and inevitably I immediately "lost" the paper with my goals written on it, or I threw it away deliberately.

The reason it does not work is because the goals must be very specific. They also have to be measurable in time and space.

If I had a goal to speak in the Philippines before I knew how to make goals properly, would I just say, "Sometime in the next five years I am going to speak in the Philippines." Now that I know how to set goals properly, I would say, "I will travel to Manila in the Philippines and hold a seminar for 1,000 people. I will have accomplished this goal by January 3, 2017 at 5:00 p.m."

A correct goal is specific: I will hold a seminar in Manila in the Philippines for 1,000 people. It is measurable: I will do it by January 3, 2017 at 5:00 p.m. I write this down as my goal. Then I know the clock is ticking and I need to make sure I take the proper steps to accomplish my goal by that time. I have until 5:00 on January 3, 2017 to accomplish my goal. If I keep this thought in front of my eyes, read it, and review the goal morning and evening, then it is going to create energy in my brain that will produce whatever I need to accomplish the goal.

My current reality is that right at the moment I am not in the Philippines, so how am I going to get there? When you have a goal, it sets things in motion for you to accomplish whatever you desire. People and opportunities will show up to help you accomplish the goal you are focused on.

## Vision Boards

Another way to begin having your thoughts move creatively is to make a vision board. This is an actual board containing a collection of pictures and objects related to what you want to have, be, or do. Place your board where you can see it every day; it has the power to activate your subconscious in helping you achieve your goals.

Vision boards are very simple to make, and they are powerful in their results. I took a tri-fold foam board that stands up by itself—like the kind kids use for science fair projects. I thought carefully about all the things I want to be, have, or do, and I found pictures on the Internet. I printed the pictures, made up some word strips, and I used words and phrases from a commercial vision board I had purchased. You can also cut out pictures from magazines.

I have a picture of Ireland and the Blarney Castle on my board because I want to go there. I want to see the Blarney Stone. I have pictures of Bora Bora, including the specific hotel where I want to stay.

I have a picture of the Philippines. I have a picture of a large conference center with my photo superimposed on the podium so it looks like I am speaking there.

I have a picture of a whole lot of cash on my vision board. There is a picture of a bunch of temples I want to visit throughout the world. There is a picture of my book. There is a picture of a pair of feet standing on a bathroom scale with the number I want to achieve and maintain as my ideal weight.

I also have words on my vision board: "abundance," "prosperity," "clarity," "success," "hope," "joy," "trust," "believe," "create," and "love."

I have a picture of the TED logo on my vision board to remind me that one of my goals is to give a TED talk.

There are also phrases on my vision board. One phrase says, "My thoughts are powerful." Others say:

> I can do anything.
> All the love I need is within me.
> I am happy and content.
> I see a world filled with love.
> I make a difference in the world.
> I am strong and healthy.
> I am divinely guided and protected.
> I attract the positive.
> My life is abundant in every way.
> I am successful.

These phrases, or affirmations, are assembled in a creative hodge-podge mess on my poster board.

I also have directly in my line of sight a picture of a $100,000 bill, because this is a goal I want to achieve—to make $100,000 in one year.

## Affirmations

An affirmation needs to be written in the present tense—not "I will" but "I am." "I am" is the most powerful phrase in the entire universe. You become what you say you are.

Take a moment and try this exercise:

Stand up and make your hands into fists. Then raise your hands above your head and say firmly out loud, "I am competent" or "I am successful." "I am beautiful" or "I am . . ." whatever you want to be.

Whenever we say negative things to ourselves, they often start with "I am." When you are getting out of the shower and you walk past the bathroom mirror, you do not usually look at yourself and say something beginning with "they are"—you say "I am." Some of the most hurtful things we say to ourselves begin with "I am."

If we change our focus and shift it so that we are saying positive things to ourselves, then the positive will become our reality.

For an affirmation, you have to *act as if*—act as if it has already happened; act as if you are already living the kind of life you desire. You need to believe it is possible. Do not worry about *how* it is going to happen. I do not know how I am going to make six figures in one year, but I *believe* it is going to happen.

In writing out your affirmation, begin with present tense—"I am"—and then write an emotion. Remember, whenever we want to make a change we have to involve all parts of our bodies, not just our thoughts, not just our brains, but we need to involve *all* of our body. Emotion gives our affirmation power.

Then we need to add an action verb that ends with "ing." For example, singing, standing, speaking, flying, hover boarding—whatever it is that you want to do. Your action will take it from being just a dream to becoming a reality.

Your affirmation needs to be brief so you can say it quickly and you can also memorize it.

As an example of how to do this using present tense, with an emotion, and the "ing" verb, here are some of my affirmations:

I am joyously reclaiming myself.
I am joyously charismatic.
I am happily worthy of notice.
I am joyfully and easily learning to play my gorgeous piano.
I am cheerfully able to pay all our bills with the great
   abundance we receive.

If you are unable to come up with an action verb ending with "ing," you can use other action verbs. Some of my other affirmations are:

I am relieved and excited that my memory and brain function are clear and acute.
I am delighted to share my talents with sold-out audiences.
I am thrilled and grateful to lead seminars with hundreds of happy attendees.
I am grateful that I have a loving, supportive and talented business team.

You can use affirmations for anything—a physical goal you want to accomplish, a health goal, or anything else. You can say that you are delighted your liver is functioning properly or that your mind is sharp and you are able to think clearly.

Do not worry about *how* your affirmation is going to become your reality. Read your affirmations at least three times a day. Read them when you get up first thing in the morning, sometime during the day, and again at night. They will make a difference because they will change the vibrational pull around your body. You will begin to see how to accomplish your dreams step by step until you manifest results.

Instead of pulling negative things towards you, affirmations will begin to pull positive things towards you—things that will cause you to have a Soul Shift within, especially if you are saying things to yourself to counteract the negative thoughts you might be tempted to say. Here are several possible, positive affirmations:

I am brilliant.
I am beautiful.
I am worth loving.
I am important.
I deserve to be safe.

CHAPTER FIFTEEN

# Be a Soul Shifter

**Definition of a Soul Shifter:** "A soul shifter is a person who is intentionally working toward a positive shift in their personality, beliefs, and behaviors with the end goal of shifting negative belief patterns and replacing them in order to experience peace, harmony, and unconditional love for themselves and all others."

## Stumbling Blocks to the Soul Shift

When you begin working towards a Soul Shift, you could encounter some difficulties. You might have an external lack of support. Perhaps the people you hang out with most do not want you to change. They like you the way you are.

If you don't change, they will not be required to change. This allows them to remain completely comfortable. However, when you begin making changes and they begin getting uncomfortable, they might withdraw their support. They might actively become hostile towards your trying to change.

You will need to determine whether or not getting rid of your pain is worth the hassle you'll have to go through to accomplish it.

Another stumbling block is internal: the lack of belief it will work. Do you believe you can change your life? Do you even *want* to believe it's possible? Can you allow yourself to have hope? If you just hang on to hope—even if you are not able to believe it right at this moment—it can work because hope can be enough.

The third stumbling block might be the lack of desire to follow through. A Soul Shift is not an easy process. Making changes in your life requires a lot of work. It involves strenuous mental, physical, and emotional effort, but it is worth it.

Do you really *desire in your heart* to change your life and make it completely different? If so, nothing will stand in your way.

The last stumbling block might be your lack of recognizing that you need to change in the first place. If you're not ready to accept 100% Responsibility, you're not ready to make changes. Perhaps you are happy keeping up the status quo. I doubt this, though, or you would not have read so far.

## Maintaining Your Soul Shift

Throughout this book, there have been suggestions about exercises you can do. Create and repeat your affirmations and goals, and surround yourself with supportive people.

Choose someone who is a good friend, who you know you can trust, and have this person become your "accountability partner." Let him (or her) know what you would like to accomplish in a day, and towards your goal of making some shift or change in your life. Ask this person to hold you accountable in a loving and compassionate way.

I took a chance and invited a stranger I had met at a conference to be my accountability partner. I knew nothing about her, but I liked her positive energy. Now she is one of my best friends.

Your daily habits need to include a gratitude journal. Write down everything you are grateful for, even if it is just feeling the wind on your face. Start with the small things if you feel like there is nothing in your life to be grateful for.

Let me tell you a true story about *tell me something good*.

Judy's second daughter, Molly, was struggling. Molly was in her first year of college, and it seemed to her that everything that could go wrong had gone wrong. She had been accepted to a college out-of-state, but she had been unable to attend because of finances. It seemed all her friends were attending this college and she felt very alone, as one by one they left for school.

Molly had also been accepted to a prestigious university in the town where she lived, but it was definitely not her preference to attend this school and live at home.

Every day, she would come home and unburden herself to her mother, who did her best to listen patiently and offer some sort of parental wisdom. Unfortunately, the negativity began to make Judy cranky and out of sorts, and she began to dread Molly's arrival at the end of the day, knowing that another tirade was on the way.

At first, Judy thought it was just a phase and Molly would get over it. She remembered what it was like to be a young adult striking out on her own, and she could empathize with the disappointment Molly felt about school. She thought perhaps Molly would be able to work through the difficulties, given a little time.

Months went by, however, and Molly did not seem to be feeling any happier about her circumstances. Instead, she seemed to spiral into depression.

One day as Molly began telling her mom about the day's horrible events, Judy thought she'd try something different. When Molly paused to take a breath before launching into the next negative, Judy said, "Now tell me something good."

Startled, Molly said, "What?"

Taking a deep breath, Judy said, "For every three bad things you tell me, you must tell me something good about your day."

Frowning, Molly sarcastically replied, "I didn't get run over by a car today."

"Good," Judy said, "Now what else happened today?"

Molly launched right back into the negatives. Judy counted. After three more negatives, she held up her hand and said, "Now tell me another good thing."

This went on for about a week. Judy would stop her daughter whenever she launched into how horrible the world was, and say, "Now tell me something good."

At first Molly's answers were sullen, as she grasped for anything that might count as a "good thing." After the first week, however, when Molly saw that Judy was not going to stop asking her to tell her something good, she began to look for good things in her day to report to her mother.

About a month later, Molly's conversations were more positive than negative, and Molly often teased Judy if she forgot to ask for something good. She was no longer depressed and her world was looking better. Every single day, she looked for something good several times a day, and it became a habit she continued even after she moved away from home.

Molly is a mother now, and she reported to Judy that she uses the same technique with her daughter. When Judy's granddaughter comes home and complains bitterly about her day, Molly says, "Now tell me something good."

Be mindful and reflective of the people you encounter and the media you consume. Question whether these choices are serving you. Are they contributing to your happiness? If not, investigate the deeper reason you choose to engage with whomever or whatever it is. You have choice. You are not required to continue doing things that do not bring you happiness. You can choose other friends and family, or get another job. The person who has the most power to make you happy and give you the life you've always dreamed is *YOU*.

Is staring at the television all day making you feel good? Is spending so much time on Facebook comparing your life to everybody else's perfection making you feel good? Does going to work and hanging out with people who sit around and complain all day make you feel good? If not, try to understand why you choose to engage with these people or activities.

## Safe Spaces

"Safe spaces" refers to groups of people who commit to maintaining a safe space so everyone can grow. It would be marvelous if we could have safe spaces everywhere in the world. Imagine groups of people getting together in homes, offices, and elsewhere, at least once a day, to provide a safe space for each other. These would be spaces where there is no gossiping, attacking, or judging anyone, and where everyone is open and accepting.

The rules for safe space groups would include: no criticizing, no complaining, no blaming, and no negativity—just love, support, and nurturing.

I have an ultimate goal that in all communities there will be groups of women who provide safe spaces for each other. This would not be a place where you would go for counseling; it would simply be a place where you could go to feel safe when you are feeling fearful or feeling shame, a place where you can express yourself and be validated and loved and accepted. Of course, if you've got a domestic violence issue, it would be best worked out elsewhere. It is important to help people be safe without endangering them.

There is a supportive online Soul Shift community at www.isoulshift.com, including a forum where you can connect with other women who are interested in growth, change, and support. If you want to connect with us, we would love to have you. It might be the only place where you get any kind of support, and we would love to provide this for you. I hope to meet you there soon.

I also run seminars and workshops throughout the United States, and internationally as well, in which groups of like-minded women who are ready to let go of their limiting beliefs can recapture their dreams and go after them with great gusto meet together to love and support each other. I would love to meet you there, too.

**REFERENCES**

## Books

*As a Man Thinketh* by James Allen; CreateSpace Independent Publishing Platform, 2016; originally published in 1903.
*The Art of Exceptional Living* by Jim Rohn; Simon & Schuster, 2003
*Bradshaw on the Family* by John Bradshaw; HCI Revised Edition, 1990
*Change Your Thinking Change Your Life: How to Unlock Your Full Potential For Success and Achievement* by Brian Tracy; Wiley, First Edition, 2005
*Chicken Soup for the Soul* by Jack Canfield; Chicken Soup for the Soul, First Edition, 2010
*Daring Greatly: How the Courage to Be Vulnerable Transforms the Way We Life, Love, Parent, and Lead* by Brené Brown; Avery, Reprint Edition, 2015
*The EFT Manual: Everyday Emotion Freedom Technique* by Gary Craig; Energy Psychology Press, First Edition, 2008
*The Emotion Code* by Dr. Bradley Nelson; Wellness Unmasked Publishing, 2007
*Feelings Buried Alive Never Die* by Karol Truman; Olympus Distributing, Revised Edition, 1991
*Happiness is a Choice* by Barry Neil Kaufman; Ballentine Books, 1994

*Healing the Shame that Binds You* by John Bradshaw; HCI Revised Edition, 2005

*Heal Your Body* by Louise Hay; Hay House, 1984

*Think and Grow Rich* by Napoleon Hill and Ross Cornwell; Mindpower Press, Restored Edition, Annotated, 2015

*The Secret Garden* by Francis Hodgson Burnett; Signet; Rei. Cen. Ed., 2003

*Seven Habits of Successful People: Powerful Lessons in Personal Change* by Stephen R. Covey; Simon & Schuster, Anniversary Edition, 2013

*The Success Principles, 10th Anniversary Edition: How to Get From Where You Are to Where You Want to Be,* by Jack Canfield and Janet Switzer; William Morrow Paperbacks, 2015

## Websites

To learn more about my seminars and workshops, go to Soul Shift, Inc., www.isoulshift.com

For information about the Adverse Childhood Experiences Study (ACEs), you can go to the website: www.acestoohigh.com for a copy of the test. There are wonderful articles and resources there, as well. You can also go directly to the website for the Center for Disease Control for the test: www.cdc.gov/violenceprevention/acestudy/index.html

For more information about tapping, check out the website of Gary Craig, the founder of Emotion Freedom Technique (EFT). http://www.emofree.com

# ABOUT THE AUTHOR

Michelle Nagel is a speaker, author, and a Certified Jack Canfield Success Principles Trainer. As a resilient survivor of child abuse, she is known as America's #1 Resilience Expert. With over 30 years teaching experience, she has worked with students of all ages, from 18 months to 104 years old.

Michelle's clients quickly discover that when they shift their mindset, their entire life begins to change. She is highly trained in a variety of modalities, and she brings this diverse background and experience to empower people to eliminate the negative impact of their past traumatic experiences, and alter their mindset and beliefs.

These modalities include the Emotion Freedom Technique (EFT), The Body Code, The Emotion Code, Specific Human Energy Nexus (SHEN) and she also has a Master Herbalist Certification. When combined with her intuition and empathy she is a powerful healer. Even when her clients came to her as a last resort after giving up on doctors (or after their doctors had given up on them), Michelle has been able to provide hope and healing for hundreds of people. Michelle was inspired to focus on mindset and beliefs after teaching 100s of students in her herbal seminars over the years, and discovering that without this piece some of them were not able to get well.

In addition to her healing work, Michelle enjoys a full and enriched life with her husband and children. In fact, with their help, she restored a house that was over 100 years old, remodeled a second house, and built a third!

While raising 4 active children, Michelle also built and ran several successful businesses working from home. She was a highly sought after medical transcriptionist, and a major insurance company relied on her for handling many of their most traumatic accident documentation.

Michelle's signature program, Women Who R.O.A.R. Win, empowers her clients to "perfect their R.O.A.R." so they can courageously speak their truth without fear, and make the impact they were meant to make in the world.

In her leisure time, Michelle has been the lead actress in plays, and enjoys singing, hiking, bike riding, and experiencing nature.

For information on workshops, seminars, or to hire Michelle to speak to your group, go to www.isoulshift.com.

www.ingramcontent.com/pod-product-compliance
Lightning Source LLC
Chambersburg PA
CBHW070103120526
44588CB00034B/2026